FAITH
GORSKY AND
LARA CLEVENGER,
MSH, RDN, CPT

# KETO DRINKS

*From Tasty Keto Coffee to Keto-Friendly*
*Smoothies, Juices, and More,*

100+ RECIPES TO BURN FAT,
INCREASE ENERGY,
AND BOOST YOUR
BRAINPOWER!

**ADAMS MEDIA**

NEW YORK   LONDON   TORONTO   SYDNEY   NEW DELHI

Adams Media
An Imprint of Simon & Schuster, Inc.
57 Littlefield Street
Avon, Massachusetts 02322

First Adams Media trade paperback edition April 2020

ADAMS MEDIA and colophon are trademarks of Simon & Schuster.

For information about special discounts for bulk purchases, please contact Simon & Schuster Special Sales at 1-866-506-1949 or business@simonandschuster.com.

The Simon & Schuster Speakers Bureau can bring authors to your live event. For more information or to book an event contact the Simon & Schuster Speakers Bureau at 1-866-248-3049 or visit our website at www.simonspeakers.com.

Interior design by Sylvia McArdle
Interior layout by Julia Jacintho
Photographs by James Stefiuk

Manufactured in the United States of America

10   9   8   7   6   5   4   3   2   1

Library of Congress Cataloging-in-Publication Data
Names: Gorsky, Faith, author. | Clevenger, Lara, author.
Title: Keto drinks / Faith Gorsky, Lara Clevenger, MSH, RDN, CPT.
Description: Avon, Massachusetts: Adams Media, 2020.
Includes index.
Identifiers: LCCN 2019053875 | ISBN 9781507212226 (pb) | ISBN 9781507212233 (ebook)
Subjects: LCSH: Beverages. | Ketogenic diet. | Low-carbohydrate diet--Recipes. | LCGFT: Cookbooks.
Classification: LCC TX815 .G67 2020 | DDC 641.2--dc23
LC record available at https://lccn.loc.gov/2019053875

ISBN 978-1-5072-1222-6
ISBN 978-1-5072-1223-3 (ebook)

# CONTENTS

## CHAPTER 4
# TEA 71

## CHAPTER 5
# JUICE 101

## CHAPTER 6

# MILKSHAKES 125

## CHAPTER 7

# BROTHS 155

# INTRODUCTION

When you are living a keto lifestyle, you know to steer clear of that slice of cake, the plate of pasta, and the bowl of sugary cereal. But it's important to remember that drinks can also contain lots of carbs! And it's not just in those milkshakes and coffee shop fraps—even drinks that are purportedly healthy, like green smoothies, are commonly loaded with added sugar. As a result, it's just as important to be mindful of your beverage choices as it is to be mindful of what you eat.

Fortunately though, no food or drink has to be off-limits when following a ketogenic diet. It's just a matter of making a few easy modifications so that the drinks you love fit into your lifestyle. With the help of *Keto Drinks*, you'll be able to do just that with more than one hundred recipes for delicious drinks that are all keto approved.

With this book, you will always have ketogenic drink ideas on hand so you can remake your favorites and never feel deprived. Inside you'll find low-calorie keto drink options, such as Iced Tea Lemonade and Apple Cider Vinegar Passionfruit Herbal Tea, as well as nutrient-dense low-carb, high-fat beverage options, like a Chocolate Peanut Butter milkshake and a Blueberry Cheesecake smoothie. You can also find savory broth recipes that can double as delicious, quick, and easy meals!

These keto drinks will easily fit into your lifestyle and will help keep your macros on-target with minimal effort on your part. With these recipes, you can enjoy all of your favorite drinks in a low-carb way so you can continue on your path to a better, healthier you!

# CHAPTER 1

# INTRODUCTION TO KETO DRINKS

Imagine low-carb, keto-friendly recipes for your favorite coffee shop drinks, such as a Blended Java Chip Frap or a Pink Drink; no-added-sugar versions of decadent milkshakes like Chocolate Peanut Butter and Strawberry; smoothies that won't spike your blood sugar and sap your energy levels, such as Blueberry Lemon, Carrot Cake, and Super Green Avocado; water infusions like Sparkling Blackberry Mint Splash and Faux Red Sangria that help you meet your daily water intake goals and also get in some added nutrients; flavorful broths, including Pho Beef Bone Broth and Garlic and Herb Vegetable Broth, that can double as quick and easy meals; and even nutritious and relaxing evening sips, like Moon Milk Nightcap and Lavender Sleepy Time Tisane. You'll find all these and more in this book!

This chapter will discuss what the keto diet is and why it's important that you make keto drinks—in addition to the obvious points that they will help you keep your macronutrients on-point, stay in ketosis, and reach your health goals. It will also go over the ingredients that you should keep stocked in your kitchen so whipping up one of these delicious keto drinks is as effortless as possible.

# WHAT IS THE KETO DIET?

A keto diet is a low-carbohydrate, moderate-protein, high-fat diet. When you reduce your intake of carbohydrates (your body's usual source of energy), your body is forced to adapt and make ketones to use for energy instead. If you're at a caloric surplus, your body will use these ketones and fatty acids for fuel; but if you're at a caloric deficit, your body will tap into its fat storage and use your existing fat for fuel.

Let's talk about what happens in your body when you eat carbs. Carbohydrate digestion occurs in the gastrointestinal tract, starting in the mouth. First, your body breaks the carbs down into glucose, then that glucose enters the bloodstream through the small intestines, causing blood glucose (blood sugar) to rise. This rise in blood sugar triggers insulin to transport glucose from your blood into your cells so it can be used as energy. When you eat more carbohydrates than your body needs for fuel, the excess is stored as fat in the form of triglycerides.

However, when your carb intake is limited, your body must turn to alternative fuel sources. First your body will use its stored glucose (called *glycogen*) from the muscle and liver. After that, it will break down fat for energy, that fat coming either from your diet or stored fat in the form of fatty acids and ketones (also called *ketone bodies*). Even when your carb intake is limited, your body still runs on a combination of glucose, ketones, and fatty acids because your body continues to produce glucose through a process called *gluconeogenesis*. Because of this, carbs are not a required macronutrient for most people.

When transitioning into a ketogenic diet, the method of transition is largely based on each individual person. Some people do well going "cold turkey" and jumping right into a strict keto diet, while others need to gradually reduce their carbohydrate intake a few weeks prior to starting a ketogenic diet to be able to succeed. Additionally, a person's motivation for starting a ketogenic lifestyle plays a role. For example, if a doctor prescribes a keto diet for someone with epilepsy they may start it sooner than someone who starts a keto diet for weight loss.

# WHAT IS KETOSIS?

Ketosis is the state of having elevated blood ketone levels, meaning that your body is now effectively burning fat for energy instead of carbohydrates. This can happen a few different ways:

- By following a very low-carb, high-fat diet
- By fasting (not eating or consuming drinks with calories)
- By prolonged strenuous exercise

When you are in ketosis, your body produces ketones to use as fuel either from the fat you eat or from the stored fat in your body. While you're in a state of nutritional ketosis, it's easier to tap into stored fat for fuel than if you were on a carbohydrate-based diet. This is because your blood sugar level isn't constantly being spiked due to carbohydrate intake, which leads to reduced hunger pangs and cravings. Because fat is so satiating, it's easier to eat at a caloric deficit and not feel deprived.

When your body is already running on fat for fuel, it will more readily tap into stored fat. This is because insulin isn't constantly being secreted, so fat-burning mode is left on. When eating at a caloric deficit while following a ketogenic diet, weight loss occurs. A big benefit of a ketogenic diet for weight loss is that you preserve more lean body mass and lose a higher percentage of fat than on a carbohydrate-based diet. Limiting carbohydrate intake forces your body to run on fat as your primary fuel source and puts you into a state of nutritional ketosis.

## WHAT ARE MACRONUTRIENTS?

Macronutrients include carbohydrates, protein, and fats. They're called *macronutrients* because they're typically consumed in large quantities and are measured in grams instead of micrograms or milligrams. Fat and protein are needed in large amounts to ensure that your body runs efficiently and to preserve lean body mass. Previously, carbohydrates were thought to be required, but now we know that isn't the case for most people because of gluconeogenesis. All of the foods that you eat contain at least one macronutrient. Carbohydrates and protein contain 4 calories (kcals) per gram, while fat contains 9 calories (kcals) per gram. On a typical ketogenic diet, the macronutrient breakdown is as follows:

- 60–75 percent of calories from fat
- 15–30 percent of calories from protein
- 5–10 percent of calories from carbohydrates

## SIGNS YOU'RE IN KETOSIS

During the first two weeks of being on the keto diet you may experience some symptoms that people refer to as the "keto flu." These symptoms may consist of the following:

- Headaches
- Chills
- Ashy skin tone
- Nausea

- Dizziness
- Brain fog
- Insomnia
- Irritability

- GI issues
- Sensitivity to light and sound

Some people say that the keto flu is your body's way of telling you that you're going through carbohydrate withdrawals, and in a way, it is. These symptoms pass the way a normal flu would pass once your body adjusts to running on ketones, which can take anywhere from three days to two weeks.

There are a few things you can do to mitigate or speed up the symptoms of the keto flu:

- Get plenty of electrolytes, in the form of bone broth, pickle juice, and so on
- Drink lots of water
- Make sure to get enough sleep
- If your doctor approves it, take magnesium and potassium supplements
- Be patient with yourself—the brain fog will eventually go away and your productivity will increase

After you've gone through the keto flu period, the good stuff starts. Positive signs that you're in ketosis include:

- Increased energy
- Increased focus
- Decreased appetite
- Improved mood
- Decreased inflammation
- Weight loss (if eating at a caloric deficit)
- Elevated blood ketone levels (beta-hydroxybutyrate [BHB])

## Tools to Test for Ketones (in Breath, Urine, and Blood)

To be successful on the keto diet, you don't need to test yourself unless you're using this diet for therapeutic purposes or a doctor recommends it. For those who want to test, there are a few ways to test whether you're in a state of nutritional ketosis, and some are more accurate than others. When you first start a keto diet, you may not want to invest over $100 for a blood or breath meter, so you may opt for ketone urine test strips. These urine test strips are very inexpensive (under $10 for one hundred strips) and test for the presence of ketone bodies, specifically the ketone acetoacetate. These strips are an indicator that your body is now producing ketones, but currently your body is excreting them through the urine. This is the first sign you're on your way to becoming fat-adapted, which means your body is using fatty acids and ketones as a primary fuel source, which is the point of a ketogenic diet.

Once you have been following a keto diet for a while and are committed, you may decide to purchase a blood glucose meter and blood ketone meter. These meters measure blood levels of the ketone beta-hydroxybutyrate (BHB), along with blood glucose. The level of ketones in your blood indicates how deep a level of ketosis you're in. Ketones and glucose have an inverse relationship, meaning when ketone levels rise, blood sugar lowers. Some diseases or conditions that are treated with a ketogenic diet may require deeper states of ketosis to be therapeutic. The higher ketone levels are, the deeper the state of nutritional ketosis. Blood meters cost between $50 to $100, and are available online. We use the Keto-Mojo meter because at this time it's a fraction of the cost per strip of other brands. This meter is available on the *Keto-Mojo* website and other online retailers.

If you have a little more money to spend, some people opt for getting a breath ketone meter. A couple popular brands are Ketonix and LEVL. The Ketonix meter costs between $150 and $250 and is available for purchase on their website. The LEVL meter is only available through the company's website for a monthly fee, which starts at $99 per month. These meters measure the amount of acetone in the breath, which is formed from the breakdown of acetoacetate (a by-product of fat metabolism), indicating that you're burning fat. (However, this doesn't necessarily mean that you're in ketosis. For example, after an intense workout it would show the presence of acetone in the breath because you're using fat for fuel during the workout although you may not be in ketosis.)

# TIPS FOR YOUR KETO JOURNEY

Because the keto diet can be tricky and very different from the standard American diet (SAD), here are a few tips to help you succeed:

- Use keto drinks as a tool to help satisfy your carb cravings while maintaining nutritional ketosis.
- Eat a variety of foods, focusing on low-carb, high-fat options such as grass-fed meat and dairy; free-range chicken and eggs; wild-caught seafood; seeds and nuts; low-carb fruits, such as berries, avocados, coconut, and olives; and low-carb vegetables, such as leafy greens, and cruciferous, nonstarchy vegetables.
- Choose top-quality healthy fats, such as grass-fed lard or tallow, coconut oil, avocado oil, olive oil, grass-fed butter, and/or ghee.
- Eat foods high in magnesium and potassium or use supplements to make sure you're getting enough electrolytes to avoid muscle cramping. Similarly, make sure you're getting 3–5 grams of sodium per day (or follow your physician's advice on sodium intake) to keep your electrolyte levels balanced. We recommend using a high-quality sea salt like Redmond Real Salt, which is typically available online or in many grocery stores.

Some people choose to use an electrolyte powder, such as Dr. Berg's Electrolyte Powder or Vega Sport Hydrator.

- Stay hydrated—water is the best way to do this! A good rule is to consume half your body weight in pounds in ounces of water.

- Get into a routine where you're meal planning and meal prepping to save time and money, and also to avoid having to resort to high-carb or fast food on busy days.

# WHY YOU SHOULD MAKE KETO DRINKS

Keto drinks are every bit as delicious (if not more so) than their non-keto counterparts. This is important because when you drink frequently throughout the day, your drink choices really matter! Take a look at your daily drink choices and you'll see how fast carbs can add up if you're not mindful of them.

It's important to note that a lot of drinks that may appear to be healthy can actually contain hidden carbs. Consider, for example, a cup of chicken broth. More often than not, sugar is an ingredient in store-bought broth! Take also green smoothies, many of which are made with just a cup of greens and then are loaded with highly sweet fruit (such as pineapple, mango, banana, and so on), and may even contain added sweeteners like honey or maple syrup. Most people whip up a green smoothie in the morning and think they're doing a great thing by getting their greens in early, but they don't really think about the quantity of sugar they're actually taking in. It's for this reason that you should have keto-friendly drink recipes at the ready.

Additionally, having keto drink options available for your favorite non-keto drinks helps you not feel deprived. When your family heads out to an ice cream stand or your friends meet up at a cafe, it's nice to be able to bring a drink along that will satisfy your cravings. In this book you'll even find soda-inspired keto drinks, including Faux Ginger Ale and Tart Cherry Vanilla.

Also, sometimes you're just so busy that the only thing you have time to whip up is a drink on your way out the door. That's not a problem at all when the drink you make is a nourishing, satiating keto drink that's nutrient-dense and full of healthy fats for fuel. We love starting the day with a Hot Butternut Coffee, ending the day with a Moon Milk Nightcap, and having one of our hot broths for lunch.

Last but not least, you will save money by making your own keto drinks! Yes, keto has become mainstream to the point where you can go to your favorite local coffeehouse and probably order a low-carb, high-fat version of your favorite drink with ease, but the cost of those drinks really adds up. Even if you just take the time to brew your own coffee or tea every morning instead of hitting up the drive-through you'll save $1,825 a year (based on ordering one drink per day with an average price of $5 per drink). Think about what you'd prefer to spend that money on!

# KETO DRINK BASICS

In terms of "ketofying" the various things you ingest, drinks are actually pretty easy! A big source of carbohydrates in drinks usually comes from sweeteners, including sugar, honey, maple syrup, and agave nectar. Sometimes it's a simple swap, like using stevia (or your preferred keto-friendly sweetener) instead of a regular sweetener when you make lemonade. Other times you have to get a little creative; for example, when making an indulgent-tasting milkshake, nixing the ice cream and using a natural thickener, such as flaxseed meal or chia seeds, paired with heavy cream and blended with ice. And occasionally, it means forgoing or at least minimizing very sugary fruit (e.g., pineapple, bananas, mango, and so on) in favor of low-carb fruit, such as blueberries and kiwi. The point is, just about any drink you enjoy can be remade into a keto-friendly version of itself.

# KETO DRINK INGREDIENTS

Like other meals on the keto diet, keto drinks should have a low-carb, moderate-protein, high-fat macronutrient profile. You achieve this through the use of healthy fats, such as grass-fed dairy, coconut milk and coconut oil, high-fat seeds and nuts, and certain high-fat fruits, such as avocados and coconut. Even though fruit is generally higher in carbs, keto drinks can still contain a variety of different fruit; it's just important to be mindful of portion sizes and weigh out your ingredients. You can also use vegetables, such as kale, spinach, celery, and even cauliflower in your drinks.

The key to creating the perfect keto drink is to find the right components that not only give you the right nutritional stats, but also create a delicious flavor profile. There are a lot of keto-friendly drink ingredients out there!

## Liquids

All smoothies need a liquid to blend properly. In its most basic form the liquid can be water, but where's the fun in that, right? Try using the liquid component of a smoothie as a way to get in more flavor and/or healthy fat. Here are a few favorites:

- **Almond milk:** Look for almond milk that only contains almonds and water, or at least a product that's unsweetened. Because so many almond milk varieties on the market contain gums (such as guar gum, xanthan gum, and so on), you can make your own almond milk when you have time. To do so, soak 1 cup of almonds in room temperature water for 12 hours. Slip off the skins, and then blend the almonds (discard the soaking liquid) with 4 cups cool water. Strain twice through cheesecloth and store in a covered glass jar up to three days in the refrigerator.

- **Canned unsweetened full-fat coconut milk:** You can find great-quality canned coconut milk on the market (look for BPA-free cans). Make sure to stir the coconut milk before measuring because the thicker, waxy portion will rise to the top and solidify.
- **Grass-fed heavy cream:** For a "near perfect" balance of fatty acids as well as health-beneficial conjugated linoleic acid (CLA), look for heavy cream (and other forms of dairy, such as ghee and butter) that is grass-fed and not just organic.
- **Coffee:** In cold drink recipes, try using cold brew coffee (you can find a recipe for it in this book). However, in fatty hot blended coffee drinks, you can use either drip coffee or French press; basically whatever you brew up for your morning cup of joe will work fine. A few recipes in this book call for espresso. If you don't have an espresso maker, you can substitute with the same amount of double-strength coffee.
- **Tea:** If you're whipping up a cold drink, use cold brew tea (you'll find out how to make it in this book). You'll also find a few hot drinks that use hot tea that's steeped the normal way. Additionally, a few recipes use matcha powder.
- **Broth:** In the chapter on fatty hot blended broth drinks (Chapter 7), you'll use beef bone broth, chicken bone broth, fish stock, and vegetable stock. Don't worry, you'll also find recipes for how to make these broths, but if you can find a great-quality store-bought brand you trust, go ahead and use that as a time-saver.

## Thickeners
A few favorite keto thickeners are chia seeds (pulsed in the blender until powdery before adding the other ingredients), protein powder (some people prefer unflavored whey protein powder so they can add their own flavor to the smoothie), flaxseed meal (golden flaxseed meal has a milder flavor than brown), nuts (such as almonds, walnuts, and pecans), blended frozen fruit (such as berries), and even pulsed-in ice. If you've been to Starbucks and ordered a blended drink, you've probably watched in amazement as they blend in ice to make it thick—you can do that at home too!

## Fats
Fat in keto drinks can come from the following:

- High-fat fruit, such as avocado
- High-fat nuts, like macadamia
- High-fat liquids, including full-fat coconut milk and grass-fed heavy cream
- High-fat seeds, such as chia and flax

## Proteins

In keto smoothies and drinks, protein usually comes in the form of protein powder, collagen peptides, and/or seeds and nuts. If you want, you can go old-school and add a raw egg to really bump up the nutrition! Just make sure the egg is pasteurized or from a local farm you trust.

## Carbs

To keep these recipes low-carb, try to avoid fruits and vegetables that are higher in carbs, as well as natural sweeteners. That is not to say these things are "unhealthy" or "not-keto"; we just want to make it as easy as possible for you to fit these smoothies into your keto macronutrient requirements.

## Fruits and Vegetables

It's important to note that even low-carb fruits and vegetables have carbs. Low-carb fruits and vegetables that feature in this book's recipes include:

- Coconut
- Berries, such as strawberries, blackberries, blueberries, and raspberries
- Watermelon
- Avocado
- Leafy greens, like spinach and kale
- Herbs, such as parsley and mint

A few recipes also use small amounts of higher-carb fruits, such as pineapple, to get the flavor profile right.

## Natural Sweeteners

Honey, coconut sugar, and maple syrup are popular natural sweeteners. Blackstrap molasses and agave nectar are also sometimes classified as natural sweeteners. However, you should try to avoid or at least minimize these products in your keto drinks because they cause a blood sugar spike and potentially contain too many carbs for an individual to consume and remain in ketosis.

# FLAVOR ENHANCERS

Just because a drink is keto doesn't mean it has to be boring! There are plenty of keto-friendly ingredients that will help you create an exciting drink that tastes as wonderful as it looks, and is full of healthy fats and low in carbs. This section will discuss some keto-friendly sweeteners, as well as extracts and essential oils, spices, and aromatics.

## Keto-Friendly Sweeteners

The recipes in this book use stevia or erythritol, or a blend of these sweeteners. Stevia sweetener comes from the *Stevia rebaudiana* plant native to South America. It's considered a "nonnutritive sweetener" because the body doesn't metabolize the active compounds in stevia, so it essentially has zero calories. Stevia can be up to two hundred times as sweet as regular sugar. Be aware that at high concentrations, stevia can have a bitter aftertaste.

Erythritol is a sugar alcohol that is created when yeast ferments glucose from corn or wheat. It is very low in calories and about 70 percent as sweet as regular sugar. Most of the erythritol that's ingested is absorbed in the bloodstream before it even reaches the colon, and is passed from the body via urine. The thing to note about erythritol is that it can have a "cooling effect," which is basically a tingly, minty aftertaste similar to menthol.

To minimize the bitterness that stevia can have and counteract erythritol's cooling effect, you should use a combination of these two sweeteners for the best flavor.

## Vanilla, Other Extracts, and Essential Oils

Whenever possible, look for "pure" extracts. Here are a few extracts and essential oils used in this book:

- Vanilla extract
- Vanilla bean paste
- Almond extract
- Hazelnut extract
- Coconut extract
- Peppermint extract
- Culinary-grade orange essential oil

## Spices and Aromatics

It's pretty incredible how something as simple as a pinch of cinnamon or a bit of fresh-grated ginger can take a drink from "just okay" to extraordinary. Here are a few spices and aromatics you should consider adding to your keto drinks:

- Warm spices, like cinnamon, nutmeg, allspice, cloves, and so on (we love the spice fenugreek because it has natural flavor notes of burnt sugar and maple)
- Fresh herbs, like mint in sweet smoothies and cilantro and/or parsley in savory smoothies
- Aromatics, including fresh ginger (for sweet drinks) and fresh garlic (for savory drinks)
- Organic fresh citrus zest, such as orange, lemon, and lime

# DRINKS WITHOUT THE GUILT

Switching to a keto diet can be a challenge, especially when you're used to drinking sweetened drinks all the time. Fortunately, the recipes in this book will provide you with low-carb, great-tasting recipes to swap out with your old sugary ones so that you can seamlessly transition into a keto or low-carb diet. The recipes will transform your former carb-loving self into a keto powerhouse!

The goal of this book is to teach you how to make fabulous keto drinks so that you can enjoy the keto lifestyle without feeling deprived. This book will help you stay on track with your keto goals and provide you with the recipes and knowledge to do so.

# CHAPTER 2

# SMOOTHIES

# ALMOND BUTTER AND JELLY

*With inspiration from a PB&J, we took that iconic sandwich and made it into a deliciously rich and creamy keto smoothie that's as popular with adults as it is with kiddos. Strawberry jam is our favorite, but feel free to use any sugar-free jam you have on hand.*

**Serves 1**

**1 cup plain unsweetened almond milk**

**2 tablespoons unsweetened creamy almond butter**

**½ tablespoon milled golden flaxseed**

**1 teaspoon vanilla extract**

**¼ teaspoon almond extract**

**10 drops liquid stevia**

**⅛ teaspoon sea salt**

**1 cup ice cubes**

**1 teaspoon sugar-free strawberry jam**

**Per Serving**
Calories: 277 | Fat: 22g
Protein: 9g | Sodium: 551mg
Fiber: 4g | Carbohydrates: 13g
Net Carbohydrates: 5g | Sugar: 3g

**1** Add the almond milk, almond butter, flaxseed, vanilla extract, almond extract, stevia, and salt to a blender and process until smooth.

**2** Add the ice cubes and pulse until thick and creamy, tamping down as necessary.

**3** Pour into a glass, stir in the strawberry jam, and serve immediately.

# BLACKBERRY COCONUT

*Sweet/tart blackberries go so well with creamy coconut. If you don't think a keto smoothie will keep you satisfied, give this one a try. With healthy fat from coconut milk and golden flaxseed, along with blackberries for fiber, this drink will keep you going all morning long.*

*Serves 1*

⅔ cup canned unsweetened full-fat coconut milk

½ tablespoon milled golden flaxseed

¾ teaspoon vanilla extract

¼ teaspoon coconut extract

⅛ teaspoon sea salt

10 drops liquid stevia

¼ cup frozen blackberries

1 cup ice cubes

**1** Add the coconut milk, flaxseed, vanilla extract, coconut extract, salt, and stevia to a blender and process until smooth.

**2** Add the frozen blackberries and ice cubes and pulse until thick and creamy, tamping down as necessary.

**3** Pour into a glass and serve immediately.

**Per Serving**
Calories: 344 | Fat: 34g | Protein: 4g | Sodium: 314mg | Fiber: 4g
Carbohydrates: 9g | Net Carbohydrates: 5g | Sugar: 2g

---

# BLACKBERRY MOJITO

*This refreshing slushy-style drink is perfect for sipping on those crazy-hot summer days. With this keto drink in one hand and a good book in the other, there's no more relaxing way to spend a lazy afternoon!*

*Serves 1*

1 tablespoon MCT oil

1 tablespoon fresh lime juice

1 teaspoon fresh lime zest

14 drops liquid stevia

1 sprig mint

¼ cup water

¼ cup frozen blackberries

½ cup crushed ice

**1** Add the MCT oil, lime juice, lime zest, stevia, mint, and water to a blender and process until smooth.

**2** Add the frozen blackberries and ice, and pulse until thick and creamy, tamping down as necessary.

**3** Pour into a glass and serve immediately.

**Per Serving**
Calories: 136 | Fat: 14g | Protein: 1g | Sodium: 4mg | Fiber: 2g
Carbohydrates: 5g | Net Carbohydrates: 3g | Sugar: 2g

# BLUEBERRY CHEESECAKE

*Is it breakfast? Is it dessert? This Blueberry Cheesecake smoothie blurs the lines! If you want, go ahead and add a pinch of ground cinnamon for even more flavor without changing the carbs.*

**Serves 1**

1 ounce cream cheese
¼ cup heavy whipping cream
½ cup water
½ teaspoon milled golden flaxseed
1 teaspoon vanilla extract
¼ teaspoon vanilla bean paste
⅛ teaspoon sea salt
12 drops liquid stevia
¼ cup frozen blueberries
1 cup ice cubes

**Per Serving**
Calories: 347 | Fat: 32g
Protein: 4g | Sodium: 400mg
Fiber: 1g | Carbohydrates: 10g
Net Carbohydrates: 9g | Sugar: 8g

**1** Add the cream cheese, cream, water, flaxseed, vanilla extract, vanilla bean paste, salt, and stevia to a blender and process until smooth.

**2** Add the frozen blueberries and ice cubes and pulse until thick and creamy, tamping down as necessary.

**3** Pour into a glass and serve immediately.

# BLUEBERRY LEMON

*This slushy-style smoothie is sure to cool you down, refresh, and recharge you on a hot day. In addition to blueberries and lemon, we add a splash of vanilla for flavor; you can also switch it up and use ⅛ teaspoon of ground cinnamon instead, without changing the carb amount.*

**Serves 1**

1 tablespoon MCT oil
1 tablespoon fresh lemon juice
1 teaspoon fresh lemon zest
14 drops liquid stevia
¼ cup water
¼ teaspoon vanilla extract
¼ cup frozen blueberries
½ cup crushed ice

**1** Add the MCT oil, lemon juice, lemon zest, stevia, water, and vanilla extract to a blender and process until smooth.

**2** Add the frozen blueberries and ice, and pulse until thick and creamy, tamping down as necessary.

**3** Pour into a glass and serve immediately.

**Per Serving**
Calories: 144 | Fat: 14g | Protein: 0g | Sodium: 4mg | Fiber: 1g
Carbohydrates: 7g | Net Carbohydrates: 6g | Sugar: 4g

---

# CITRUS MATCHA

*The fresh flavors of lemon and lime pack a punch in this keto smoothie! You can also add 1 teaspoon of orange zest to bump up the bright citrusy flavor even more. Or you can add grapefruit zest if that's your thing. Take whatever citrus zest you like and put your own spin on this delicious drink.*

**Serves 1**

⅔ cup canned unsweetened full-fat coconut milk
½ tablespoon milled golden flaxseed
¾ teaspoon powdered matcha
1 teaspoon fresh lime zest
1 teaspoon fresh lemon zest
½ teaspoon fresh lemon juice
⅛ teaspoon sea salt
10 drops liquid stevia
1 cup ice cubes

**1** Add the coconut milk, flaxseed, matcha, lime zest, lemon zest, lemon juice, salt, and stevia to a blender and process until smooth.

**2** Add the ice cubes and pulse until thick and creamy, tamping down as necessary.

**3** Pour into a glass and serve immediately.

**Per Serving**
Calories: 322 | Fat: 34g | Protein: 5g | Sodium: 314mg | Fiber: 3g
Carbohydrates: 6g | Net Carbohydrates: 3g | Sugar: 0g

# CHOCOLATE MATCHA

*At first glance, chocolate and matcha might sound like an odd pairing, but their earthiness blends surprisingly well! Be sure to use unsweetened cocoa powder; we recommend natural cocoa powder instead of Dutch-processed.*

**Serves 1**

⅔ cup canned unsweetened full-fat coconut milk

1 tablespoon unsweetened cocoa powder

½ tablespoon milled golden flaxseed

¾ teaspoon powdered matcha

1 teaspoon vanilla extract

¼ teaspoon fresh lemon juice

⅛ teaspoon sea salt

12 drops liquid stevia

1 cup ice cubes

**Per Serving**
Calories: 359 | Fat: 35g
Protein: 6g | Sodium: 315mg
Fiber: 4g | Carbohydrates: 9g
Net Carbohydrates: 5g | Sugar: 1g

**1** Add the coconut milk, cocoa powder, flaxseed, matcha, vanilla extract, lemon juice, salt, and stevia to a blender and process until smooth.

**2** Add the ice cubes and pulse until thick and creamy, tamping down as necessary.

**3** Pour into a glass and serve immediately.

**Can You Use Cacao Powder Instead of Cocoa Powder?**

Yes! Cacao powder will give this a slightly different flavor, but if you like how cacao powder tastes, you'll enjoy it in this smoothie. The beans used to make cacao powder are processed at much lower temperatures and therefore retain a higher amount of minerals and nutrients versus cocoa powder. Cacao powder does have a slightly more bitter flavor, but the nutritional content is superior.

# CARROT CAKE

*Coconut, walnuts, cinnamon, and a hint of carrot make this keto smoothie taste just like cake. Now, we're not saying this should replace your birthday dessert (because you deserve actual cake on your birthday!), but if you want to have your cake and eat it too for breakfast, this smoothie is the way to go.*

Serves 1

**1 tablespoon shelled walnuts**

**⅔ cup canned unsweetened full-fat coconut milk**

**¾ teaspoon vanilla extract**

**½ teaspoon ground cinnamon**

**⅛ teaspoon sea salt**

**8 drops liquid stevia**

**1 tablespoon shredded carrot**

**1 cup ice cubes**

**Per Serving**
Calories: 360 | Fat: 37g
Protein: 4g | Sodium: 317mg
Fiber: 3g | Carbohydrates: 7g
Net Carbohydrates: 4g | Sugar: 1g

**1** Add the walnuts to a blender and pulse until powdery.

**2** Add the coconut milk, vanilla extract, cinnamon, salt, and stevia to the blender and process until smooth. Add the shredded carrot and pulse a couple times until finely chopped.

**3** Add the ice cubes and pulse until thick and creamy, tamping down as necessary.

**4** Pour into a glass and serve immediately.

# CRANBERRY ORANGE

*Around the holidays, this is one of our favorite flavor profiles. Tart cranberries, bright orange zest, and just a hint of cinnamon will have you humming holiday music. Make a big batch and whip it up as part of a festive holiday brunch. Your guests will love it and never even guess it is keto!*

**Serves 1**

1 tablespoon toasted almonds

¼ cup heavy whipping cream

½ cup water

1 teaspoon milled golden flaxseed

12 drops liquid stevia

1½ teaspoons fresh orange zest

1 teaspoon vanilla extract

½ teaspoon vanilla bean paste

⅛ teaspoon ground cinnamon

⅛ teaspoon sea salt

½ tablespoon low-sugar dried cranberries

1 cup ice cubes

**Per Serving**
Calories: 288 | Fat: 26g
Protein: 3g | Sodium: 311mg
Fiber: 2g | Carbohydrates: 10g
Net Carbohydrates: 8g | Sugar: 7g

**1** Add the almonds to a blender and pulse until powdery.

**2** Add the cream, water, flaxseed, stevia, orange zest, vanilla extract, vanilla bean paste, cinnamon, salt, and dried cranberries to the blender and process until smooth (a few flecks of cranberries are fine).

**3** Add the ice cubes and pulse until thick and creamy, tamping down as necessary.

**4** Pour into a glass and serve immediately.

**Where Can You Find Low-Sugar Dried Cranberries?**

You can find brands like Ocean Spray Craisins Dried Cranberries 50% Less Sugar at your regular grocery store. They're also available online.

# COCONUT VANILLA KIWI

*Kiwi bumps up the nutrition of this coconut-based keto smoothie. It features both vanilla extract and vanilla bean paste for an intense vanilla flavor and aroma. You can add up to 1 cup of baby spinach leaves to this one and probably won't even taste it!*

**Serves 1**

⅔ cup canned unsweetened full-fat coconut milk
¾ teaspoon vanilla extract
¼ teaspoon coconut extract
¼ teaspoon vanilla bean paste
⅛ teaspoon sea salt
8 drops liquid stevia
½ medium kiwi, peeled and chopped
1 cup ice cubes

**1** Add the coconut milk, vanilla extract, coconut extract, vanilla bean paste, salt, stevia, and kiwi to a blender and process until smooth.

**2** Add the ice cubes and pulse until thick and creamy, tamping down as necessary.

**3** Pour into a glass and serve immediately.

**Per Serving**
Calories: 336 | Fat: 32g | Protein: 3g | Sodium: 313mg | Fiber: 3g
Carbohydrates: 11g | Net Carbohydrates: 8g | Sugar: 4g

---

# COCONUT VANILLA MATCHA

*This smoothie is sure to become your new favorite way to enjoy matcha if you want all the benefits of matcha with a taste that is a little sweeter and more mellow. The combination of coconut and vanilla marries perfectly with the bright flavor of matcha. Whip this up as part of your morning routine for an energizing start to your day.*

**Serves 1**

⅔ cup canned unsweetened full-fat coconut milk
½ tablespoon milled golden flaxseed
¾ teaspoon powdered matcha
1 teaspoon vanilla extract
¼ teaspoon coconut extract
⅛ teaspoon sea salt
12 drops liquid stevia
1 cup ice cubes

**1** Add the coconut milk, flaxseed, matcha, vanilla extract, coconut extract, salt, and stevia to a blender and process until smooth.

**2** Add the ice cubes and pulse until thick and creamy, tamping down as necessary.

**3** Pour into a glass and serve immediately.

**Per Serving**
Calories: 336 | Fat: 34g | Protein: 5g | Sodium: 314mg | Fiber: 3g
Carbohydrates: 6g | Net Carbohydrates: 3g | Sugar: 1g

# CHOCOLATE-COVERED STRAWBERRY

*If you like Neapolitan ice cream with strawberry, chocolate, and vanilla, this is the drink for you because it has all three of those flavors going on. To make it even more special, you can dip a fresh strawberry in 90% dark chocolate, let the chocolate harden, and use that as a garnish.*

**Serves 1**

¼ cup heavy whipping cream

½ cup water

1 tablespoon unsweetened cocoa powder

1 teaspoon milled golden flaxseed

12 drops liquid stevia

1½ teaspoons vanilla extract

⅛ teaspoon sea salt

½ cup frozen chopped strawberries

½ cup ice cubes

½ teaspoon 90% dark chocolate shavings, for garnish

**Per Serving**
Calories: 280 | Fat: 24g
Protein: 4g | Sodium: 313mg
Fiber: 4g | Carbohydrates: 14g
Net Carbohydrates: 9g | Sugar: 6g

**1** Add the cream, water, cocoa powder, flaxseed, stevia, vanilla extract, and salt to a blender and process until smooth.

**2** Add the frozen strawberries and ice cubes and pulse until thick and creamy, tamping down as necessary.

**3** Pour into a glass, sprinkle the chocolate shavings on top, and serve immediately.

# GINGER MATCHA

*Zippy ginger adds a real kick to this matcha smoothie! You should use fresh ginger for the most intense pop of ginger flavor, but in a pinch you can substitute ½ teaspoon of dried ginger instead.*

Serves 1

⅔ cup canned unsweetened full-fat coconut milk

½ tablespoon milled golden flaxseed

¾ teaspoon powdered matcha

1 teaspoon grated fresh ginger

½ teaspoon fresh lemon juice

⅛ teaspoon sea salt

10 drops liquid stevia

1 cup ice cubes

**1** Add the coconut milk, flaxseed, matcha, ginger, lemon juice, salt, and stevia to a blender and process until smooth.

**2** Add the ice cubes and pulse until thick and creamy, tamping down as necessary.

**3** Pour into a glass and serve immediately.

**Per Serving**
Calories: 323 | Fat: 34g | Protein: 5g | Sodium: 314mg | Fiber: 3g
Carbohydrates: 6g | Net Carbohydrates: 3g | Sugar: 0g

---

# MINTED MATCHA

*Using coconut milk as the base for this and other matcha smoothies helps mellow out the intensity that matcha can have. Here, grassy matcha is brightened with fresh mint in this invigorating keto smoothie! We recommend using fresh mint leaves for this, but if you can't find them you could substitute ¼ teaspoon of mint extract instead.*

Serves 1

⅔ cup canned unsweetened full-fat coconut milk

10 fresh mint leaves

½ tablespoon milled golden flaxseed

¾ teaspoon powdered matcha

1 teaspoon vanilla extract

½ teaspoon fresh lemon juice

⅛ teaspoon sea salt

12 drops liquid stevia

1 cup ice cubes

**1** Add the coconut milk, mint leaves, flaxseed, matcha, vanilla extract, lemon juice, salt, and stevia to a blender and process until smooth.

**2** Add the ice cubes and pulse until thick and creamy, tamping down as necessary.

**3** Pour into a glass and serve immediately.

**Per Serving**
Calories: 334 | Fat: 34g | Protein: 5g | Sodium: 314mg | Fiber: 3g
Carbohydrates: 6g | Net Carbohydrates: 3g | Sugar: 1g

# GREEN GINGERED CITRUS SUNSHINE

*We both live in Florida and wanted to commemorate the Sunshine State with the bright flavors of citrus in this smoothie. With fresh orange and lemon zest, as well as ginger, this keto smoothie tastes like (green) sunshine! It has a bright, invigorating aroma and packs a punch of flavor to go along with it.*

**Serves 1**

⅔ cup canned unsweetened full-fat coconut milk

½ tablespoon milled golden flaxseed

½ teaspoon lemon juice

1 teaspoon lemon zest

1 teaspoon orange zest

¾ teaspoon grated fresh ginger

⅛ teaspoon sea salt

10 drops liquid stevia

1 cup fresh baby spinach leaves

1 cup ice cubes

**Per Serving**
Calories: 327 | Fat: 34g
Protein: 5g | Sodium: 338mg
Fiber: 4g | Carbohydrates: 8g
Net Carbohydrates: 4g | Sugar: 0g

**1** Add the coconut milk, flaxseed, lemon juice, lemon zest, orange zest, ginger, salt, stevia, and spinach to a blender and process until smooth.

**2** Add the ice cubes and pulse until thick and creamy, tamping down as necessary.

**3** Pour into a glass and serve immediately.

## How Should You Grate Fresh Ginger?

Break or cut a small (about ½"–1") chunk of ginger off a gingerroot. Use a metal spoon to scrape off the ginger peel (the skin is so thin you don't need to use a knife). Grate the ginger using a very small grater or preferably a microplane.

# GREEN MATCHA MACHINE

*With spinach, avocado, and coconut milk, this verdant smoothie is a powerhouse of nutrition! If you struggle with getting in all your vegetables at lunch and dinner, whip this up for breakfast and get your greens in early.*

**Serves 1**

½ cup canned unsweetened full-fat coconut milk

¼ cup water

1 cup fresh baby spinach leaves

¼ medium avocado, peeled, pitted, and sliced

¾ teaspoon powdered matcha

½ teaspoon fresh lemon juice

⅛ teaspoon sea salt

12 drops liquid stevia

1 cup ice cubes

**Per Serving**
Calories: 316 | Fat: 32g
Protein: 6g | Sodium: 335mg
Fiber: 5g | Carbohydrates: 9g
Net Carbohydrates: 4g | Sugar: 1g

**1** Add the coconut milk, water, spinach, avocado, matcha, lemon juice, salt, and stevia to a blender and process until smooth.

**2** Add the ice cubes and pulse until thick and creamy, tamping down as necessary.

**3** Pour into a glass and serve immediately.

## Can You Taste the Spinach?

Fresh baby spinach leaves are fairly mild tasting, so their flavor doesn't come through all that much in this smoothie. However, the avocado flavor and texture is ever so slightly more noticeable. If you're new to green smoothies and worried that you won't like the flavor, you can always start with fewer greens and work your way up.

# SUPER GREEN AVOCADO

*With lemon and parsley, this gorgeous green smoothie is great for detox! Mint adds a subtle sweetness to balance out the kale, so the flavor isn't too overwhelming. This smoothie is loaded with antioxidants and fiber, and we like to whip it up for breakfast about once a week.*

**Serves 1**

⅔ cup canned unsweetened full-fat coconut milk

1 teaspoon lemon juice

1 teaspoon lemon zest

⅛ teapoon sea salt

10 drops liquid stevia

1 cup chopped kale

¼ medium avocado, peeled, pitted, and sliced

3 sprigs fresh parsley

1 sprig fresh mint

1 cup ice cubes

**Per Serving**
Calories: 390 | Fat: 40g
Protein: 5g | Sodium: 324mg
Fiber: 6g | Carbohydrates: 11g
Net Carbohydrates: 5g | Sugar: 1g

**1** Add the coconut milk, lemon juice, lemon zest, salt, stevia, kale, avocado, parsley, and mint to a blender and process until smooth.

**2** Add the ice cubes and pulse until thick and creamy, tamping down as necessary.

**3** Pour into a glass and serve immediately.

## Kale and Vitamin K

This super green smoothie packs a wallop of nutrition! It's made with kale, avocado, and parsley. For vitamin K, it meets 140 percent of the recommended dietary allowance (RDA) for men and 188 percent of the RDA for women. Vitamin K is important for blood clotting and bone metabolism. If you're on blood thinner medication, check with your doctor before eating ingredients rich in vitamin K, such as kale.

# GOLDEN TURMERIC COCONUT

*Black pepper might seem like a strange smoothie ingredient, but it helps improve the bioavailability of turmeric. Meaning that it helps your body better obtain and use all of turmeric's anti-inflammatory benefits. If you like golden milk lattes, you'll love this pretty golden smoothie!*

Serves 1

⅔ cup canned unsweetened full-fat coconut milk

½ tablespoon milled golden flaxseed

¾ teaspoon vanilla extract

¼ teaspoon coconut extract

½ teaspoon ground turmeric

⅛ teaspoon ground black pepper

⅛ teaspoon sea salt

10 drops liquid stevia

1 cup ice cubes

**Per Serving**
Calories: 332 | Fat: 34g
Protein: 4g | Sodium: 314mg
Fiber: 3g | Carbohydrates: 7g
Net Carbohydrates: 4g | Sugar: 1g

**1** Add the coconut milk, flaxseed, vanilla extract, coconut extract, turmeric, black pepper, salt, and stevia to a blender and process until smooth.

**2** Add the ice cubes and pulse until thick and creamy, tamping down as necessary.

**3** Pour into a glass and serve immediately.

# KALE KIWI

*This keto smoothie packs a natural punch of vitamins A, K, and C, thanks to the kale-kiwi blend. It's the perfect mixture of tangy and sweet flavors, and a great way to refuel after a workout.*

**Serves 1**

1 cup chopped kale

½ medium kiwi, peeled and chopped

⅔ cup canned unsweetened full-fat coconut milk

1 teaspoon fresh lemon zest

½ teaspoon fresh lemon juice

⅛ teaspoon sea salt

12 drops liquid stevia

1 cup ice cubes

**Per Serving**
Calories: 328 | Fat: 32g
Protein: 4g | Sodium: 320mg
Fiber: 4g | Carbohydrates: 11g
Net Carbohydrates: 8g | Sugar: 4g

**1** Add the kale, kiwi, coconut milk, lemon zest, lemon juice, salt, and stevia to a blender and process until smooth.

**2** Add the ice cubes and pulse until thick and creamy, tamping down as necessary.

**3** Pour into a glass and serve immediately.

## Which Kale Should You Buy?

Curly kale or red kale both work great in smoothies; just be sure to de-stem them first. If you're looking for something milder in flavor, baby kale leaves are the way to go.

# SALTED CHOCOLATE MACADAMIA

*Intensely rich and decadent, this keto smoothie almost tastes like brownie batter in liquid form. Coconut milk adds subtle sweetness and depth of flavor here, but if you prefer heavy cream you can use $\frac{1}{4}$ cup heavy whipping cream with $\frac{1}{2}$ cup water instead.*

Serves 1

**1 tablespoon unsalted macadamia nuts**

**⅔ cup canned unsweetened full-fat coconut milk**

**1 tablespoon unsweetened cocoa powder**

**¾ teaspoon vanilla extract**

**¼ teaspoon coconut extract**

**⅛ teaspoon sea salt**

**12 drops liquid stevia**

**1 cup ice cubes**

**Pinch flaky sea salt, for garnish**

**Per Serving**
Calories: 395 | Fat: 40g
Protein: 5g | Sodium: 315mg
Fiber: 4g | Carbohydrates: 9g
Net Carbohydrates: 5g | Sugar: 1g

**1** Add the macadamia nuts to a blender and pulse until powdery.

**2** Add the coconut milk, cocoa powder, vanilla extract, coconut extract, salt, and stevia to the blender and process until smooth.

**3** Add the ice cubes and pulse until thick and creamy, tamping down as necessary.

**4** Pour into a glass, sprinkle the flaky sea salt on top, and serve immediately.

# TROPICAL MACADAMIA COCONUT

*The high fat content and buttery texture of macadamia nuts adds richness and depth to this deliciously satiating keto smoothie! If you can't find unsalted macadamia nuts, just use salted nuts and omit the sea salt.*

Serves 1

**1 tablespoon unsalted macadamia nuts**
**⅔ cup canned unsweetened full-fat coconut milk**
**¾ teaspoon vanilla extract**
**¼ teaspoon coconut extract**
**⅛ teapoon sea salt**
**10 drops liquid stevia**
**1 cup ice cubes**

**Per Serving**
Calories: 369 | Fat: 38g
Protein: 4g | Sodium: 313mg
Fiber: 2g | Carbohydrates: 6g
Net Carbohydrates: 4g | Sugar: 1g

**1** Add the macadamia nuts to a blender and pulse until powdery.

**2** Add the coconut milk, vanilla extract, coconut extract, salt, and stevia to the blender and process until smooth.

**3** Add the ice cubes and pulse until thick and creamy, tamping down as necessary.

**4** Pour into a glass and serve immediately.

# PIÑA COLADA

*There's nothing like a piña colada to give you a real taste of the tropics! Blend up this keto smoothie, and you'll feel like you wandered onto a beach. Of course, if you're whipping this up for adults only, you can add a splash of rum if you want.*

**Serves 1**

¼ cup chopped fresh pineapple

⅔ cup canned unsweetened full-fat coconut milk

1 teaspoon milled golden flaxseed

1 teaspoon vanilla extract

¼ teaspoon coconut extract

⅛ teaspoon sea salt

6 drops liquid stevia

1 cup ice cubes

**Per Serving**
Calories: 345 | Fat: 33g
Protein: 4g | Sodium: 313mg
Fiber: 3g | Carbohydrates: 11g
Net Carbohydrates: 8g | Sugar: 5g

**1** Add the pineapple, coconut milk, flaxseed, vanilla extract, coconut extract, salt, and stevia to a blender and process until smooth.

**2** Add the ice cubes and pulse until thick and creamy, tamping down as necessary.

**3** Pour into a glass and serve immediately.

# CHAPTER 3

# COFFEE

# BLENDED CASHEW VANILLA COFFEE

*Cashews, vanilla, and Homemade Keto Caramel add nutty notes of caramel to this blended coffee beverage. This one is equally delicious made with coconut milk instead of heavy whipping cream.*

**Serves 1**

**1 tablespoon raw unsalted cashews**
**¾ cup cold brew coffee**
**3 tablespoons heavy whipping cream**
**3 tablespoons water**
**2 tablespoons Homemade Keto Caramel (see sidebar on this page)**
**1 teaspoon vanilla extract**
**8 drops liquid stevia**
**1 cup ice cubes**

**Per Serving**
Calories: 331 | Fat: 32g
Protein: 4g | Sodium: 52mg
Fiber: 0g | Carbohydrates: 7g
Net Carbohydrates: 5g | Sugar: 3g

**1** Add the cashews to a blender and pulse until powdery.

**2** Add the cold brew coffee, cream, water, Homemade Keto Caramel, vanilla extract, and stevia to the blender and process until smooth.

**3** Add the ice cubes and pulse until thick and creamy, tamping down as necessary.

**4** Pour into a glass and serve immediately.

## How to Make Homemade Keto Caramel

To make about 1 cup of your own smooth and buttery keto caramel you'll need: 4 tablespoons unsalted butter, 2 tablespoons granulated erythritol, 1 cup heavy whipping cream, ½ teaspoon vanilla extract, ¼ teaspoon cream of tartar, ⅛ teaspoon stevia glycerite, and ⅛ teaspoon sea salt. Add the butter and granulated erythritol to a medium saucepan over medium heat. Bring to a boil and then cook until it turns light brown, about 3–4 minutes, swirling the saucepan occasionally. Next, add the cream, vanilla extract, cream of tartar, stevia glycerite, and salt. Bring to a boil, and then cook until the sauce is thickened slightly (it should coat the back of a wooden spoon), about 3 minutes. Finally, cool the caramel to room temperature (it will thicken more as it cools), and then store in a glass jar covered in the refrigerator up to two weeks.

# BLENDED COCONUT CARAMEL COFFEE

*For an energizing taste of the tropics, you're going to love this Blended Coconut Caramel Coffee! We use canned unsweetened full-fat coconut milk for creamy texture and flavor, and we bump up the coconut even more with a splash of coconut extract.*

**Serves 1**

¾ cup cold brew coffee

3 tablespoons canned unsweetened full-fat coconut milk

3 tablespoons water

2 tablespoons Homemade Keto Caramel (see Blended Cashew Vanilla Coffee recipe in this chapter)

1 teaspoon milled golden flaxseed

½ teaspoon vanilla extract

½ teaspoon coconut extract

10 drops liquid stevia

1 cup ice cubes

**Per Serving**
Calories: 224 | Fat: 22g
Protein: 2g | Sodium: 46mg
Fiber: 1g | Carbohydrates: 5g
Net Carbohydrates: 2g | Sugar: 1g

**1** Add the cold brew coffee, coconut milk, water, Homemade Keto Caramel, flaxseed, vanilla extract, coconut extract, and stevia to a blender and process until smooth.

**2** Add the ice cubes and pulse until thick and creamy, tamping down as necessary.

**3** Pour into a glass and serve immediately.

# BLENDED COLD BREW

*This Blended Cold Brew has deep coffee flavor and serves as the starting point for a lot of coffee-based keto drinks! You can use a good-quality store-bought cold brew that you like, or easily make your own. You can use regular coffee in this recipe, but because of the way that cold brew coffee is prepared, it gives a highly concentrated coffee flavor and less bitterness that really adds to this drink.*

**Serves 1**

¾ cup cold brew coffee
¼ cup heavy whipping cream
1 teaspoon milled golden flaxseed
10 drops liquid stevia
1 cup ice cubes

**1** Add the cold brew coffee, cream, flaxseed, and stevia to a blender and process until smooth.

**2** Add the ice cubes and pulse until thick and creamy, tamping down as necessary.

**3** Pour into a glass and serve immediately.

**Per Serving**
Calories: 219 | Fat: 23g
Protein: 2g | Sodium: 23mg
Fiber: 1g | Carbohydrates: 2g
Net Carbohydrates: 2g | Sugar: 2g

**Make Your Own Cold Brew**

To make your own cold brew, combine 1½ cups filtered water with ⅓ cup medium-ground good-quality coffee in a medium glass bowl. Cover it and let it sit at room temperature up to 24 hours. Double strain the liquid through a fine mesh sieve or cheesecloth-lined sieve. Store your cold brew concentrate in the refrigerator up to one month.

# BUTTER COFFEE

*This classic favorite is for real coffee lovers. The flavor of coffee shines through, and it's complemented with a gorgeous foamy cap and rich texture. Be sure to use a great-quality coffee that you love the flavor of!*

**Serves 1**

**1 cup strong brewed hot coffee**
**1½ tablespoons unsalted butter**
**½ tablespoon MCT oil**

**1** Add all ingredients to a blender and process until smooth.

**2** Serve.

**Per Serving**
Calories: 213 | Fat: 24g | Protein: 0g | Sodium: 7mg | Fiber: 0g
Carbohydrates: 0g | Net Carbohydrates: 0g | Sugar: 0g

---

# HOT BUTTERNUT COFFEE

*Butter, vanilla, and almond come together for a rich, buttery, and nutty coffee experience. We add just a hint of stevia for sweetness, but you can omit it or add more to suit your preference. If you're a fan of Harry Potter, you can think of this drink as the hot, caffeinated keto version of Butterbeer!*

**Serves 1**

**1 cup strong brewed hot coffee**
**1½ tablespoons unsalted butter**
**¾ teaspoon vanilla extract**
**¼ teaspoon almond extract**
**3 drops liquid stevia**

**1** Add all ingredients to a blender and process until smooth.

**2** Serve.

**Per Serving**
Calories: 167 | Fat: 17g | Protein: 0g | Sodium: 8mg | Fiber: 0g
Carbohydrates: 0g | Net Carbohydrates: 0g | Sugar: 0g

# BUTTERED HAZELNUT ESPRESSO

*Nutty with a hint of vanilla, this is the perfect way to start your day. The blended butter gives it a nice foamy top, which makes it look like a latte. If you have an espresso machine at home, use a double shot of espresso and ½ cup of hot water instead of the brewed coffee.*

Serves 1

**1 cup strong brewed hot coffee**
**1½ tablespoons unsalted butter**
**½ teaspoon vanilla extract**
**½ teaspoon hazelnut extract**
**5 drops liquid stevia**

**Per Serving**
Calories: 167 | Fat: 17g
Protein: 0g | Sodium: 8mg
Fiber: 0g | Carbohydrates: 0g
Net Carbohydrates: 0g | Sugar: 0g

**1** Add all ingredients to a blender and process until smooth.

**2** Serve immediately.

## Can You Use Whole Hazelnuts?

If you have a high-speed blender, you can use 1 tablespoon whole hazelnuts and omit the hazelnut extract. Be warned: You may still get small bits of hazelnuts in your coffee.

# BLENDED PISTACHIO CHOCOLATE CHIP COFFEE

*With the pistachio-chocolate-coffee flavor combination, you'll feel like you're enjoying gelato paired with an espresso from your favorite Italian ice cream shop with this blended coffee treat! You can switch up the flavor profile here by using any kind of nut extract you like; almond is also delicious.*

**Serves 1**

**¾ cup cold brew coffee**
**¼ cup heavy whipping cream**
**1 teaspoon milled golden flaxseed**
**½ teaspoon pistachio extract**
**10 drops liquid stevia**
**1 cup ice cubes**
**1 tablespoon stevia-sweetened chocolate chips**

**1** Add the cold brew coffee, cream, flaxseed, pistachio extract, and stevia to a blender and process until smooth.

**2** Add the ice cubes and pulse until thick and creamy, tamping down as necessary. Add the chocolate chips and pulse a few times.

**3** Pour into a glass and serve immediately.

**Per Serving**
Calories: 295 | Fat: 27g
Protein: 3g | Sodium: 23mg
Fiber: 2g | Carbohydrates: 11g
Net Carbohydrates: 3g | Sugar: 2g

## Can You Use Pistachios Instead?

Yes! You can use 1 tablespoon unsalted shelled pistachios in this recipe (blended in with the liquids) if you want to omit the pistachio extract.

# BLENDED TOASTED ALMOND COFFEE

*Who knew that toasted almonds are the key to easily amping up the flavor of a blended coffee drink?! The toasted nuttiness of almonds pulls out the roasted, toasty notes in coffee for a combination that's even more delicious than it sounds. If you don't have slivered almonds, you can use sliced or whole, just be sure to toast them in a dry skillet on the stovetop first to maximize their nutty flavor.*

**Serves 1**

**1 tablespoon toasted slivered almonds**
**¾ cup cold brew coffee**
**¼ cup heavy whipping cream**
**8 drops liquid stevia**
**1 cup ice cubes**

**Per Serving**
Calories: 239 | Fat: 25g
Protein: 3g | Sodium: 21mg
Fiber: 1g | Carbohydrates: 3g
Net Carbohydrates: 2g | Sugar: 2g

**1** Add almonds to a blender and pulse them until powdery.

**2** Add the cold brew coffee, cream, and stevia to the blender and process until smooth.

**3** Add the ice cubes and pulse until thick and creamy, tamping down as necessary.

**4** Pour into a glass and serve immediately.

## Are All Store-Bought Cold Brew Coffees the Same?

No! Surprisingly, we've noticed a pretty big variation in how strong (and also sometimes how bitter) different brands of store-bought cold brew coffee can be. Because of this, you may want to adjust the amount of stevia, and you may want to dilute the coffee with water if it's very strong.

# BLENDED CINNAMON DOLCE FRAP

*Look out, Starbucks, there's a new Cinnamon Dolce in town! It's thick, rich, creamy, and full of flavor. You won't miss the carbs here at all. If you're not a huge fan of cinnamon, skip this one, but for the cinnamon-lovers, this will be your new favorite drink.*

**Serves 1**

¾ cup cold brew coffee

¼ cup heavy whipping cream

1 teaspoon milled golden flaxseed

½ teaspoon vanilla extract

½ teaspoon ground cinnamon

10 drops liquid stevia

1 cup ice cubes

**Per Serving**
Calories: 228 | Fat: 23g
Protein: 2g | Sodium: 23mg
Fiber: 1g | Carbohydrates: 4g
Net Carbohydrates: 2g | Sugar: 2g

**1** Add the cold brew coffee, cream, flaxseed, vanilla extract, cinnamon, and stevia to a blender and process until smooth.

**2** Add the ice cubes and pulse until thick and creamy, tamping down as necessary.

**3** Pour into a glass and serve immediately.

# BLENDED PECAN CARAMEL TURTLE COFFEE

*With the flavors of chocolate, pecan, and caramel, this blended coffee-based keto drink was made with turtle candy–lovers in mind! To make this treat even more decadent, serve it garnished with a dollop of whipped cream, a drizzle of Homemade Keto Caramel, and a sprinkle of dark chocolate shavings.*

**Serves 1**

**1 tablespoon shelled pecans**

**¾ cup cold brew coffee**

**3 tablespoons heavy whipping cream**

**3 tablespoons water**

**2 tablespoons Homemade Keto Caramel (see Blended Cashew Vanilla Coffee recipe in this chapter)**

**½ tablespoon unsweetened cocoa powder**

**½ teaspoon vanilla extract**

**10 drops liquid stevia**

**1 cup ice cubes**

**Per Serving**
Calories: 328 | Fat: 34g
Protein: 3g | Sodium: 52mg
Fiber: 2g | Carbohydrates: 7g
Net Carbohydrates: 3g | Sugar: 2g

**1** Add the pecans to a blender and pulse until powdery.

**2** Add the cold brew coffee, cream, water, Homemade Keto Caramel, cocoa powder, vanilla extract, and stevia to the blender and process until smooth.

**3** Add the ice cubes and pulse until thick and creamy, tamping down as necessary.

**4** Pour into a glass and serve immediately.

# BLENDED JAVA CHIP FRAP

*If you love the combination of coffee and chocolate as much as we do, you'll end up making this Blended Java Chip Frap at home instead of heading out to a coffee shop to buy it. If you enjoy the flavor of bitter chocolate, you can use cacao nibs instead of stevia-sweetened chocolate chips.*

**Serves 1**

¾ cup cold brew coffee
¼ cup heavy whipping cream
1 teaspoon milled golden flaxseed
½ teaspoon vanilla extract
10 drops liquid stevia
1 cup ice cubes
1 tablespoon stevia-sweetened chocolate chips

**1** Add the cold brew coffee, cream, flaxseed, vanilla extract, and stevia to a blender and process until smooth.

**2** Add the ice cubes and pulse until thick and creamy, tamping down as necessary.

**3** Add the chocolate chips and pulse a couple times to break them up.

**4** Pour into a glass and serve immediately.

**Per Serving**
Calories: 295 | Fat: 27g | Protein: 3g | Sodium: 23mg | Fiber: 2g
Carbohydrates: 12g | Net Carbohydrates: 3g | Sugar: 2g

---

# HOT PEPPERMINT MOCHA LATTE

*You don't have to wait for the holidays to make this Hot Peppermint Mocha Latte! It tastes like a chocolate-covered candy cane was melted into your latte. The potency of different brands of peppermint extract can vary, so if you aren't sure how strong yours is, add a little less at first and then add more to suit your tastes.*

**Serves 1**

1 cup strong brewed hot coffee
1 tablespoon unsalted butter
½ tablespoon MCT oil
½ tablespoon unsweetened cocoa powder
½ teaspoon vanilla extract
¼ teaspoon peppermint extract
8 drops liquid stevia

**1** Add all ingredients to a blender and process until smooth.

**2** Serve immediately.

**Per Serving**
Calories: 184 | Fat: 19g | Protein: 1g | Sodium: 9mg | Fiber: 1g
Carbohydrates: 2g | Net Carbohydrates: 1g | Sugar: 0g

# TURMERIC LATTE

Also called a Golden Milk Latte, or just Golden Milk, this keto drink is caffeine-free and soothing. Turmeric is known for its anti-inflammatory properties, and the black pepper in this drink helps your body absorb the turmeric.

**Serves 1**

1 cup simmering plain unsweetened almond milk

1 tablespoon unsalted butter

½ tablespoon MCT oil

½ teaspoon vanilla extract

½ teaspoon ground turmeric

¼ teaspoon ground cinnamon

¼ teaspoon ground ginger

¼ teaspoon ground black pepper

7 drops liquid stevia

**Per Serving**
Calories: 213 | Fat: 21g
Protein: 2g | Sodium: 190mg
Fiber: 1g | Carbohydrates: 4g
Net Carbohydrates: 3g | Sugar: 0g

**1** Add all ingredients to a blender and process until smooth.

**2** Serve.

# HOT CARDAMOM COFFEE

*Inspired by classic Turkish coffee, the coffee should be strong and this drink should be quite aromatic with cardamom. If possible, we recommend using freshly ground cardamom for the most intense flavor.*

**Serves 1**

**1 cup strong brewed hot coffee**
**1½ tablespoons unsalted butter**
**½ tablespoon MCT oil**
**⅛ teaspoon ground green cardamom**

**Per Serving**
Calories: 213 | Fat: 24g
Protein: 0g | Sodium: 7mg
Fiber: 0g | Carbohydrates: 0g
Net Carbohydrates: 0g | Sugar: 0g

**1** Add all ingredients to a blender and process until smooth.

**2** Serve immediately.

## What Does Cardamom Taste Like?

Cardamom has a complex flavor and aroma. It's a cooling spice, and has somewhat of a menthol, eucalyptus-like effect. It also has notes of piquancy, as well as mint.

# HOT CINNAMON LATTE

*Spiced with cinnamon and laced with nutmeg, this foam-topped coffee looks like a latte and is a completely satisfying way to start the day. We don't add any sweetener, but if you prefer your coffee on the sweet side, feel free to add a couple drops of liquid stevia to suit your tastes.*

**Serves 1**

**1 cup strong brewed hot coffee**
**1 tablespoon unsalted butter**
**½ tablespoon MCT oil**
**½ teaspoon ground cinnamon**
**⅛ teaspoon ground nutmeg**

**Per Serving**
Calories: 166 | Fat: 19g
Protein: 0g | Sodium: 6mg
Fiber: 1g | Carbohydrates: 1g
Net Carbohydrates: 0g | Sugar: 0g

**1** Add all ingredients to a blender and process until smooth.

**2** Serve.

---

**Saigon Cinnamon vs. Ceylon Cinnamon**

Saigon cinnamon isn't actually cinnamon; rather, it's from a closely related tree called *cassia*. Ceylon cinnamon is considered "real" cinnamon, and has a slightly sweeter, subtler flavor.

# HOT EGGNOG LATTE

*Aromatic with nutmeg and a touch of vanilla, this coffee-based hot beverage will remind you of your favorite festive holiday drink. You can also make this classic without coffee; to do so, skip the coffee and butter, increase the heavy whipping cream to 4 tablespoons, and add ¾ cup hot water.*

**Serves 1**

**1 cup strong brewed hot coffee**
**1 tablespoon unsalted butter**
**1 tablespoon heavy whipping cream**
**½ teaspoon vanilla extract**
**⅛ teaspoon ground nutmeg**
**5 drops liquid stevia**

**1** Add all ingredients to a blender and process until smooth.

**2** Serve.

**Per Serving**
Calories: 163 | Fat: 17g | Protein: 1g | Sodium: 12mg | Fiber: 0g
Carbohydrates: 1g | Net Carbohydrates: 1g | Sugar: 1g

---

# HOT MAPLE LATTE

*The smoky sweetness of stevia-sweetened maple-flavored syrup is a surprisingly fantastic pairing with coffee. If you prefer not to use maple-flavored syrup, you can instead use ⅛–¼ teaspoon ground fenugreek with liquid stevia to taste for a similar flavor profile.*

**Serves 1**

**1 cup strong brewed hot coffee**
**1 tablespoon stevia-sweetened maple-flavored syrup**
**1 tablespoon unsalted butter**
**½ tablespoon MCT oil**
**¼ teaspoon vanilla extract**

**1** Add all ingredients to a blender and process until smooth.

**2** Serve.

**Per Serving**
Calories: 200 | Fat: 19g | Protein: 0g | Sodium: 21mg | Fiber: 0g
Carbohydrates: 8g | Net Carbohydrates: 8g | Sugar: 0g

# HOT MOCHA COFFEE

*Hot chocolate or coffee? Rich and chocolatey, this Hot Mocha Coffee is the best of both worlds. Butter gives it a gorgeous frothy top, but if you prefer you can skip the butter and use 2 tablespoons of heavy whipping cream instead.*

Serves 1

**1 cup strong brewed hot coffee**
**1 tablespoon unsalted butter**
**1 tablespoon heavy whipping cream**
**½ tablespoon unsweetened cocoa powder**
**½ teaspoon vanilla extract**
**7 drops liquid stevia**

**Per Serving**
Calories: 175 | Fat: 18g
Protein: 1g | Sodium: 13mg
Fiber: 1g | Carbohydrates: 2g
Net Carbohydrates: 1g | Sugar: 1g

**1** Add all ingredients to a blender and process until smooth.

**2** Serve immediately.

### What's the Difference Between Natural and Dutch-Processed Cocoa Powder?

When making Dutch-processed cocoa powder, the cacao beans are treated with alkali to neutralize their natural acidity. As a result, Dutch-processed cocoa powder has a milder chocolate flavor and is less acidic than natural cocoa powder. Because of their difference in acidity (which affects interaction with leaveners), these two kinds of cocoa powder are not interchangeable in baking. However, when making smoothies you can use whichever you prefer or have on hand. Generally, we prefer natural cocoa powder because of the flavor and the fact that it's slightly less processed.

# HOT PUMPKIN SPICE LATTE

*Now you can make a keto-friendly version of that ubiquitous fall drink right in your own home. And the best part? You'll love it as much as the version you get from your local coffee shop.*

**Serves 1**

**1 cup strong brewed hot coffee**

**1 tablespoon unsweetened pumpkin purée**

**1 tablespoon unsalted butter**

**½ tablespoon MCT oil**

**½ teaspoon pumpkin pie spice mix**

**¼ teaspoon vanilla extract**

**7 drops liquid stevia**

*Per Serving*
Calories: 173 | Fat: 19g
Protein: 1g | Sodium: 9mg
Fiber: 1g | Carbohydrates: 2g
Net Carbohydrates: 1g | Sugar: 1g

**1** Add all ingredients to a blender and process until smooth.

**2** Serve.

## What's in Pumpkin Pie Spice Mix?

Pumpkin pie spice mix usually contains a blend of the following: cinnamon, ginger, nutmeg, allspice, and cloves.

# HOT VANILLA LATTE

*Subtly sweet and aromatic with vanilla, this latte-like drink feels fancy but only requires minimal effort! If you enjoy the energizing benefits of butter coffee, but want to switch up the flavor profile to keep things interesting, this drink is the way to go.*

**Serves 1**

**1 cup strong brewed hot coffee**
**1 tablespoon unsalted butter**
**½ tablespoon MCT oil**
**½ teaspoon vanilla extract**
**3 drops liquid stevia**

**Per Serving**
Calories: 168 | Fat: 19g
Protein: 0g | Sodium: 7mg
Fiber: 0g | Carbohydrates: 0g
Net Carbohydrates: 0g | Sugar: 0g

**1** Add all ingredients to a blender and process until smooth.

**2** Serve.

## Making Your Own Extract

To make your own vanilla extract, combine 1 liter of vodka with 10 vanilla beans that are split lengthwise in a sealed glass jar. Let it sit in a cool, dark place for at least one month, shaking it at least once a week. The longer you let it sit, the stronger the vanilla flavor will be.

# ICED VIETNAMESE COFFEE

*For the most authentic version of this drink, use dark roast Vietnamese-grown coffee brewed with a small metal Vietnamese drip filter. Sweetened condensed milk is a classic addition but is not keto approved, so we use Homemade Keto Caramel. A generous splash of heavy whipping cream adds creamy texture and richness.*

Serves 1

**1 cup cold brew coffee**

**3 tablespoons heavy whipping cream**

**2 tablespoons Homemade Keto Caramel (see Blended Cashew Vanilla Coffee recipe in this chapter)**

**1 cup ice cubes**

Per Serving
Calories: 269 | Fat: 29g
Protein: 2g | Sodium: 50mg
Fiber: 0g | Carbohydrates: 4g
Net Carbohydrates: 2g | Sugar: 2g

**1** Stir together the cold brew coffee, cream, and Homemade Keto Caramel in a glass.

**2** Stir in the ice cubes, and serve immediately.

# ICED CHOCOLATE COFFEE

*This drink will remind you of your childhood—it tastes like chocolate milk! The coffee provides a nice balance and depth of flavor, but if you don't normally like a coffee-based drink you might actually enjoy this one because of the chocolate milk flavor. If you have a sweet tooth and have the room in your macros for the day, add a sprinkle of cocoa powder or shaved chocolate to the top.*

Serves 1

**1 cup cold brew coffee**
**¼ cup heavy whipping cream**
**1 tablespoon unsweetened cocoa powder**
**10 drops liquid stevia**
**1 cup ice cubes**

**Per Serving**
Calories: 233 | Fat: 23g
Protein: 3g | Sodium: 24mg
Fiber: 2g | Carbohydrates: 5g
Net Carbohydrates: 3g | Sugar: 2g

**1** Add the cold brew coffee, cream, cocoa powder, and stevia to a blender and process until smooth.

**2** Pour into a glass, add the ice cubes, and serve immediately.

# CHAPTER 4

# TEA

# BLENDED CHAI BLACK TEA

*Black tea with its perfect blend of spices is the base of this blended tea-based drink. We simplified the process by using chai tea bags, but you can use black tea steeped with chai spices if you prefer.*

**Serves 1**

1 cup water

2 chai black tea bags

¼ cup canned unsweetened full-fat coconut milk

½ tablespoon chia seeds

¼ teaspoon vanilla extract

¼ teaspoon ground chai spice mix

⅛ teaspoon sea salt

12 drops liquid stevia

1 cup ice cubes

**Per Serving**
Calories: 142 | Fat: 14g
Protein: 2g | Sodium: 302mg
Fiber: 3g | Carbohydrates: 5g
Net Carbohydrates: 2g | Sugar: 0g

**1** In a small saucepan, bring the water to a boil and then pour it into a mug. Add the tea bags and let them steep 1 hour. Chill the tea.

**2** To a blender add ¾ cup chilled chai tea, coconut milk, chia seeds, vanilla extract, chai spice mix, salt, and stevia. Process until smooth.

**3** Add the ice cubes and pulse until thick and creamy, tamping down as necessary.

**4** Pour into a glass and serve immediately.

**What Spices Are in Chai Spice Mix?**

Chai spice mix is usually a blend of the following spices: cinnamon, cardamom, ginger, allspice, and black pepper.

# CARAMEL ROOIBOS

*Sweet homemade caramel blends well with the earthy, slightly sweet flavor of rooibos tea. We recommend brewing the rooibos extra strong for the deepest flavor in this keto drink.*

**Serves 1**

**1 cup strong brewed hot rooibos tea**

**2 tablespoons Homemade Keto Caramel (see Blended Cashew Vanilla Coffee recipe in Chapter 3)**

**½ tablespoon unsalted butter**

**1** Add all ingredients to a blender and process until smooth.

**2** Serve.

**Per Serving**
Calories: 167 | Fat: 18g | Protein: 1g | Sodium: 37mg | Fiber: 0g
Carbohydrates: 3g | Net Carbohydrates: 1g | Sugar: 1g

---

# CHAMOMILE TEA

*Relax and unwind with a good book and a hot cup of frothy Chamomile Tea in the evening. Just two ingredients make this drink quick and easy, but feel free to play with the flavor here and add a pinch of cinnamon or a splash of vanilla.*

**Serves 1**

**1 cup strong brewed hot chamomile herbal tea**

**1 tablespoon unsalted butter**

**1** Add all ingredients to a blender and process until smooth.

**2** Serve.

**Per Serving**
Calories: 104 | Fat: 12g | Protein: 0g | Sodium: 4mg | Fiber: 0g
Carbohydrates: 0g | Net Carbohydrates: 0g | Sugar: 0g

# LAVENDER SLEEPY TIME TISANE

*If you're looking for a nighttime routine to help you settle your mind and unwind after a busy day, brew up a steaming cup of this keto-friendly Lavender Sleepy Time Tisane. You can add a couple drops of liquid stevia if you prefer a sweeter brew.*

**Serves 1**

**1 cup strong brewed hot chamomile herbal tea**

**1 tablespoon unsalted butter**

**¼ teaspoon vanilla extract**

**2 drops food-grade lavender extract**

**1** Add all ingredients to a blender and process until smooth.

**2** Serve immediately.

**Per Serving**
Calories: 107 | Fat: 12g
Protein: 0g | Sodium: 4mg
Fiber: 0g | Carbohydrates: 1g
Net Carbohydrates: 1g | Sugar: 0g

## What Is a Tisane?

*Tisane* is another name for an herbal tea. Basically, it's spices or herbs (not tea) that are steeped in water for a flavorful tea-like drink. Tisanes are caffeine-free, so they're a great choice in the evening or in the morning if you're trying to reduce your coffee intake.

# BLUEBERRY WHITE ICED TEA

*White tea is a nice change from the stronger-flavored black and green teas. White tea is delicate and pairs well with the fruity flavor of berries. For a stronger flavor, you can use 2 tea bags instead of 1.*

Serves 1

**1 cup water**
**1 white tea bag**
**1 tablespoon MCT oil**
**3 drops liquid stevia**
**¼ cup fresh blueberries**
**1 cup ice cubes**

*Per Serving*
Calories: 136 | Fat: 14g
Protein: 0g | Sodium: 1mg
Fiber: 1g | Carbohydrates: 5g
Net Carbohydrates: 5g | Sugar: 4g

**1** In a small saucepan, bring the water to a boil and then pour it into a mug. Add the tea bag and let it steep 1 hour. Chill the tea.

**2** Remove the tea bag and add the tea, MCT oil, stevia, and blueberries to a blender and process until smooth.

**3** Pour into a glass and add ice cubes. Serve immediately.

## What Is White Tea?

Like black tea and green tea, white tea is made from the *Camellia sinensis* plant. However, white tea is minimally processed, and isn't rolled or oxidized, which results in a milder, more delicate flavor.

# BLUEBERRY LEMON KOMBUCHA

*This refreshing iced kombucha is a good balance of sweet/tart flavor. We usually mince the blueberries, but you could muddle or purée them as well. If you don't have lemon extract, you can add $\frac{1}{4}$–$\frac{1}{2}$ teaspoon fresh lemon zest instead.*

**Serves 1**

**1 cup unflavored kombucha**

**2 tablespoons minced fresh blueberries**

**$\frac{1}{8}$ teaspoon lemon extract**

**4 drops liquid stevia**

**$\frac{1}{2}$ cup ice cubes**

**Per Serving**
Calories: 33 | Fat: 0g
Protein: 0g | Sodium: 20mg
Fiber: 0g | Carbohydrates: 8g
Net Carbohydrates: 7g | Sugar: 6g

**1** Gently stir together all ingredients in a glass.

**2** Serve.

# MINT TEA MCT

*The soothing flavor of mint shines through in this relaxing hot keto drink. For the caffeinated version, add a green or black tea bag along with a mint tea bag when you brew it up.*

**Serves 1**

**1 cup strong brewed hot mint herbal tea**

**1 tablespoon MCT oil**

**Per Serving**
Calories: 117 | Fat: 14g
Protein: 0g | Sodium: 2mg
Fiber: 0g | Carbohydrates: 0g
Net Carbohydrates: 0g | Sugar: 0g

**1** Add all ingredients to a blender and process until smooth.

**2** Serve.

## How Much MCT Oil Is Too Much?

If you're new to MCT oil, we recommend starting with 1 teaspoon and gradually working your way up from there. See how well your body tolerates it, because if you're not used to it, MCT oil can cause digestive distress.

# MINTED BLACK ICED TEA

*Have you heard of sun tea? It's just black tea with fresh mint that's steeped in a glass jug in the sun and then served over ice. It's a summertime favorite! This Minted Black Iced Tea has the same flavor profile but with added MCT oil for fuel.*

**Serves 1**

1 cup water
1 black tea bag
1 sprig fresh mint
1 tablespoon MCT oil
5 drops liquid stevia
1 cup ice cubes

**Per Serving**
Calories: 118 | Fat: 14g
Protein: 0g | Sodium: 8mg
Fiber: 0g | Carbohydrates: 1g
Net Carbohydrates: 1g | Sugar: 0g

**1** In a small saucepan, bring the water to a boil and then pour it into a mug. Add the tea bag and mint sprig and let it steep 1 hour. Chill the tea.

**2** Remove the tea bag and mint sprig, and add the tea, MCT oil, and stevia to a blender and process until smooth.

**3** Pour into a glass and add ice cubes. Serve immediately.

## How to Make Cold Brew Tea

You can also make a cold brew tea in advance so that making this drink is quick and easy. To make your own cold brew tea: Combine 4 cups filtered water with 4 tea bags in a glass jar. Cover and refrigerate 12 hours or overnight. Remove the tea bags and store in the refrigerator up to one week.

# DETOX "ICED TEA"

*Herbal with fruity notes of lemon and apple, this Detox "Iced Tea" is a great way to help you get in your daily water intake. If you don't mind green drinks feel free to blend the water, stevia, apple cider vinegar, lemon juice, parsley, mint, and sea salt, and serve that over ice with fresh lemon slices. There's no need to let the water infuse if you blend it!*

**Serves 1**

**1½ cups water**
**7 drops liquid stevia**
**½ tablespoon apple cider vinegar**
**1 teaspoon fresh lemon juice**
**3 sprigs fresh parsley**
**1 sprig fresh mint**
**⅛ teaspoon sea salt**
**½ cup ice cubes**
**2 slices fresh lemon**

**1** Add the water, stevia, apple cider vinegar, lemon juice, parsley, mint, and salt to a glass.

**2** Cover the glass and put it in the refrigerator for 4 hours (or overnight) so the herbs can infuse the water.

**3** If desired, remove the herbs before serving. Transfer the liquid to a serving glass and add the ice and lemon slices.

**4** Serve.

**Per Serving**
Calories: 4 | Fat: 0g
Protein: 0g | Sodium: 294mg
Fiber: 0g | Carbohydrates: 1g
Net Carbohydrates: 1g | Sugar: 0g

# STRAWBERRY ROOIBOS ICED TEA

*Rooibos tea is reddish in color with a sweet, earthy flavor. Strawberries add sweetness and play up the pretty color of this herbal keto drink.*

**Serves 1**

1 cup water
1 rooibos tea bag
1 tablespoon MCT oil
3 drops liquid stevia
¼ cup fresh sliced strawberries
1 cup ice cubes

**Per Serving**
Calories: 131 | Fat: 14g
Protein: 0g | Sodium: 3mg
Fiber: 1g | Carbohydrates: 4g
Net Carbohydrates: 3g | Sugar: 2g

**1** In a small saucepan, bring the water to a boil and then pour it into a mug. Add the tea bag and let it steep 1 hour. Chill the tea.

**2** Remove the tea bag and then add the tea, MCT oil, stevia, and strawberries to a blender and process until smooth.

**3** Pour into a glass and add the ice cubes. Serve immediately.

## Is Rooibos Tea Caffeine-Free?

Yes, rooibos is native to South Africa, and it comes from a different plant than green, black, and white tea. The leaves of the rooibos plant are used to make a caffeine-free herbal brew.

# THAI ICED TEA

*Spiced and fragrant, there's nothing quite like Thai Iced Tea! It's similar to chai, but with its own unique flavor profile. If you prefer evaporated milk, you can use that instead of whipping cream (but be mindful of the carb count).*

Serves 1

**1 cup plus 2 tablespoons water**
**1 cinnamon stick**
**1 whole star anise**
**2 pods green cardamom, cracked open**
**2 whole cloves**
**½ teaspoon dried lemongrass**
**1 black tea bag**
**12 drops liquid stevia**
**1 cup crushed ice**
**3 tablespoons heavy whipping cream**

Per Serving
Calories: 156 | Fat: 16g
Protein: 2g | Sodium: 19mg
Fiber: 0g | Carbohydrates: 1g
Net Carbohydrates: 1g | Sugar: 1g

**1** To a medium saucepan, add the water, cinnamon stick, star anise, cardamom, cloves, and lemongrass. Bring mixture to a boil, and allow to boil 2 minutes. Turn off the heat, add the tea bag, cover the saucepan, and let the spices and tea steep 1 hour.

**2** Stir in the stevia and refrigerate until fully chilled.

**3** Pour into a glass along with the ice and cream. Stir and serve.

# CHAI ALMOND COOKIE

*Almond extract, a bit of extra cinnamon, and a hint of sweetness lend a cookie-like flavor to this keto version of a classic chai latte. If you want a non-caffeinated version of this drink, steep chai spices in hot water instead of using a chai black tea bag.*

**Serves 1**

1 cup strong brewed hot chai black tea

1½ tablespoons canned unsweetened full-fat coconut milk

½ tablespoon MCT oil

¼ teaspoon almond extract

⅛ teaspoon ground cinnamon

5 drops liquid stevia

### Per Serving
Calories: 106 | Fat: 12g
Protein: 0g | Sodium: 11mg
Fiber: 0g | Carbohydrates: 2g
Net Carbohydrates: 1g | Sugar: 0g

**1** Add all ingredients to a blender and process until smooth.

**2** Serve.

# APPLE CIDER VINEGAR PASSIONFRUIT HERBAL TEA

*This drink is pretty in pink and a great way to stay hydrated! You can swap out the apple cider vinegar for fresh lemon juice if you prefer.*

**Serves 1**

**1 cup water**
**1 passionfruit herbal tea bag**
**7 drops liquid stevia**
**½ teaspoon apple cider vinegar**
**½ cup ice cubes**
**1 fresh lemon slice**

**Per Serving**
Calories: 3 | Fat: 0g
Protein: 0g | Sodium: 4mg
Fiber: 0g | Carbohydrates: 1g
Net Carbohydrates: 1g | Sugar: 0g

**1** In a small saucepan, bring the water to a boil and then pour it into a mug. Add the tea bag and let it steep 1 hour. Chill the tea and then remove the tea bag.

**2** Add the tea, stevia, apple cider vinegar, ice cubes, and lemon slice to a glass, and stir.

**3** Serve.

## What Is Passionfruit Tea?

Passionfruit tea blends are usually available with or without caffeine, and they frequently contain hibiscus. The flavor of passionfruit tea is fruity, floral, and often citrusy, and it is typically a bright pink color. Personally, we like to use Tazo Passion herbal tea.

# VANILLA PINEAPPLE KOMBUCHA

*This drink is sweet enough, but not overly so, and even just using a tiny little bit of pineapple adds delicious tropical flavor. (Be sure to measure the pineapple so you know exactly how many carbs you're getting so you can keep your macros on-point.) Because it's mellow, it's a great one to start with if you've never had kombucha before!*

Serves 1

1 cup unflavored kombucha
2 tablespoons minced fresh pineapple
¼ teaspoon vanilla extract
3 drops liquid stevia
½ cup ice cubes

**1** Gently stir together all ingredients in a glass.

**2** Serve.

**Per Serving**
Calories: 32 | Fat: 0g | Protein: 0g | Sodium: 20mg | Fiber: 0g
Carbohydrates: 8g | Net Carbohydrates: 8g | Sugar: 6g

---

# ICED TEA LEMONADE

*Otherwise known as an "Arnold Palmer," this keto-approved drink is for those of us who can't decide whether we want iced tea or lemonade! It's refreshingly tart with fresh lemon and complex with black tea. You can use a different kind of tea here if you don't like black.*

Serves 1

1 cup water
1 black tea bag
8 drops liquid stevia
1 teaspoon fresh lemon juice
2 slices fresh lemon
½ cup ice cubes

**1** In a small saucepan, bring the water to a boil and then pour it into a mug. Add the tea bag and let it steep 1 hour. Chill the tea and then remove the tea bag.

**2** Add the tea, stevia, lemon juice, lemon slices, and ice to a glass, and stir.

**3** Serve.

**Per Serving**
Calories: 4 | Fat: 0g | Protein: 0g | Sodium: 9mg | Fiber: 0g
Carbohydrates: 1g | Net Carbohydrates: 1g | Sugar: 0g

# MOON MILK NIGHTCAP

*This keto drink is a beautiful shade of blue thanks to butterfly pea flower tea, which tastes similar to green tea. (You can purchase it online.) For the pink version, use passionfruit herbal tea instead of butterfly pea flower tea, and use ⅛ teaspoon rosewater instead of the vanilla extract.*

**Serves 1**

**1 cup strong brewed hot butterfly pea flower herbal tea**

**¼ cup canned unsweetened full-fat coconut milk**

**½ teaspoon vanilla extract**

**3 drops liquid stevia**

**¼ teaspoon ashwagandha powder**

**Per Serving**
Calories: 123 | Fat: 12g
Protein: 1g | Sodium: 12mg
Fiber: 1g | Carbohydrates: 3g
Net Carbohydrates: 2g | Sugar: 0g

**1** Add all ingredients to a blender and process until smooth.

**2** Serve immediately.

## What Is Ashwagandha?

Ashwagandha powder is derived from a plant in the nightshade family. It is also known by other names such as Indian ginseng and winter cherry. It's an adaptogen that is thought to have a calming, relaxing effect.

# SMASHED BLACKBERRY BLACK TEA

*Blackberries are a beautiful complement to the natural fruity notes of black tea. To add a touch of complexity to this keto drink, steep the tea with 1 whole clove and then remove it before serving.*

**Serves 1**

**1 cup water**
**1 black tea bag**
**¼ cup fresh blackberries**
**5 drops liquid stevia**
**½ cup ice cubes**

**Per Serving**
Calories: 18 | Fat: 0g
Protein: 1g | Sodium: 9mg
Fiber: 2g | Carbohydrates: 4g
Net Carbohydrates: 2g | Sugar: 2g

**1** In a small saucepan, bring the water to a boil and then pour it into a mug. Add the tea bag and let it steep 1 hour. Chill the tea and then remove the tea bag.

**2** Add the blackberries to a glass and muddle them or mash them with a fork.

**3** Add the tea, stevia, and ice to the glass with the muddled blackberries, and stir.

**4** Serve.

# SMASHED RASPBERRY GREEN TEA

*For those of you who have heard about the health benefits of green tea but don't love the flavor, start with this drink! Red raspberries add sweet/tart fruitiness to the green tea flavor, and lemon brightens it up.*

**Serves 1**

**1 cup water**
**1 green tea bag**
**¼ cup fresh red raspberries**
**6 drops liquid stevia**
**½ cup ice cubes**
**1 fresh lemon slice**

**Per Serving**
Calories: 19 | Fat: 0g
Protein: 1g | Sodium: 4mg
Fiber: 2g | Carbohydrates: 4g
Net Carbohydrates: 2g | Sugar: 1g

**1** In a small saucepan, bring the water to a boil and then pour it into a mug. Add the tea bag and let it steep 1 hour. Chill the tea and then remove the tea bag.

**2** Add the raspberries to a glass and muddle them or mash them with a fork.

**3** Add the tea, stevia, ice cubes, and lemon slice to the glass with the muddled raspberries, and stir.

**4** Serve.

# BLENDED GREEN TEA COCONUT

*If you like the slightly grassy flavor of green tea, you'll love it in this refreshing blended drink! Coconut milk mellows the earthiness of the green tea in this keto drink, and fresh lemon zest brightens it up.*

Serves 1

**1 cup water**

**2 green tea bags**

**¼ cup canned unsweetened full-fat coconut milk**

**½ tablespoon milled golden flaxseed**

**¼ teaspoon lemon zest**

**12 drops liquid stevia**

**1 cup ice cubes**

### Per Serving
Calories: 133 | Fat: 14g
Protein: 2g | Sodium: 13mg
Fiber: 2g | Carbohydrates: 3g
Net Carbohydrates: 1g | Sugar: 0g

**1** In a small saucepan, bring the water to a boil and then pour it into a mug. Add the tea bags and let them steep 1 hour. Chill the tea.

**2** In a blender, add ¾ cup chilled tea, coconut milk, flaxseed, lemon zest, and stevia and process until smooth.

**3** Add the ice cubes and pulse until thick and creamy, tamping down as necessary.

**4** Pour into a glass and serve immediately.

# WHITE DRINK

*There's just something about the peach and vanilla combination that screams summer. For this keto drink we also add coconut milk for a touch of richness and creamy texture. It almost tastes like peach ice cream in drink form. This one was inspired by the White Drink from Starbucks' secret menu, and we think you'll like it even more.*

**Serves 1**

**1 cup water**
**2 herbal peach tea bags**
**¼ cup canned unsweetened full-fat coconut milk**
**¾ teaspoon vanilla extract**
**5 drops liquid stevia**
**½ cup ice cubes**

**Per Serving**
Calories: 123 | Fat: 12g
Protein: 1g | Sodium: 11mg
Fiber: 1g | Carbohydrates: 3g
Net Carbohydrates: 2g | Sugar: 0g

**1** In a small saucepan, bring the water to a boil and then pour it into a mug. Add the tea bags and let it steep 1 hour. Chill the tea.

**2** Remove the tea bags and then add the tea, coconut milk, vanilla extract, and stevia to a blender and process until smooth.

**3** Pour into a glass and add the ice cubes. Serve immediately.

## Why Do You Blend This Drink?

We recommend blending this drink because coconut milk can be quite lumpy. To make sure the drink is smooth in texture, we recommend giving it a quick blend.

# PINK DRINK

*This blushing-shade-of-pink drink is fruity and slightly floral with a strawberry and coconut flavor. You can choose to not blend this drink, but blending smooths out any large chunks in the coconut milk.*

Serves 1

1½ cups water

2 passionfruit herbal tea bags

¼ cup canned unsweetened full-fat coconut milk

½ teaspoon vanilla extract

7 drops liquid stevia

¾ cup ice cubes

2 tablespoons freeze-dried strawberries, or 2 medium fresh strawberries, thinly sliced

Per Serving
Calories: 133 | Fat: 12g
Protein: 1g | Sodium: 13mg
Fiber: 1g | Carbohydrates: 5g
Net Carbohydrates: 4g | Sugar: 2g

**1** In a small saucepan, bring water to a boil and then pour it into a mug. Add the tea bags and let steep 1 hour. Chill the tea and then remove the tea bags.

**2** In a blender, add the tea, coconut milk, vanilla extract, and stevia and blend until smooth.

**3** Pour the drink into a glass, stir in the ice and strawberries, and serve.

# GREEN TEA KOMBUCHA BASE

*Don't freak out when you see that this recipe calls for sugar! Yes, you need the whole amount, and yes, this is still keto. The reason being, as the tea ferments, the "scoby" consumes most of the sugar. For the starter tea you can use unpasteurized, unflavored kombucha from your last batch or from the grocery store.*

**Yields 4 quarts**

**1 gallon water**
**1 cup sugar**
**8 green tea bags**
**2 cups unpasteurized, unflavored kombucha (from the last batch or store-bought)**
**1 scoby (from the last batch or store-bought)**

Per Serving (1 cup)
Calories: 30 | Fat: 0g
Protein: 0g | Sodium: 10mg
Fiber: 0g | Carbohydrates: 7g
Net Carbohydrates: 7g | Sugar: 6g

**1** In a large stockpot, bring the water to a boil, and then add the sugar and stir to dissolve. Turn off the heat.

**2** Add the tea bags and steep until the tea is cooled to room temperature. Remove and discard the tea bags.

**3** Pour the tea into a 1-gallon glass jar. Add the 2 cups kombucha. Gently add the scoby.

**4** Cover the opening of the jar with a piece of cloth and secure it with a rubber band.

**5** Let the tea ferment at room temperature in a dark place about seven to ten days. Start testing at day six or seven, and use a straw to draw up liquid to taste the kombucha. The kombucha is done fermenting when it has a balanced sweet/tart flavor.

**6** To let the kombucha carbonate, transfer the kombucha to glass bottles, leaving about 1½" at the top of each bottle before capping. At this point you can add any flavorings you like, such as fruit, herbs, spices, and so on. Again, store the kombucha at room temperature in a dark place. It generally takes about three days to carbonate.

**7** Once the kombucha is carbonated, transfer it to the refrigerator. It should stay good for about one month.

## What's a Scoby?

To make this recipe you'll need a scoby. *Scoby* is actually an acronym for "symbiotic culture of bacteria and yeast." Basically, a scoby is a slightly rubbery home for bacteria to live that floats on top of your kombucha and also protects the fermenting kombucha from outside bad bacteria. If you've made kombucha before you can use the scoby from making your last batch, or you can purchase one online. Or, if you're feeling adventurous, you can make a scoby. Search online for useful articles on how to make a scoby from scratch. Happy brewing!

# RED RASPBERRY ICED ROOIBOS TEA

*Red raspberries are a beautiful complement to the red hue of rooibos. Instead of muddling the berries, you can leave them whole and use them as is, or freeze them and use less ice cubes.*

**Serves 1**

**1 cup water**
**1 rooibos tea bag**
**4 drops liquid stevia**
**¼ cup fresh red raspberries, muddled a bit**
**1 cup ice cubes**

**Per Serving**
Calories: 19 | Fat: 0g
Protein: 0g | Sodium: 4mg
Fiber: 2g | Carbohydrates: 4g
Net Carbohydrates: 2g | Sugar: 1g

**1** In a small saucepan, bring the water to a boil and then pour it into a mug. Add the tea bag and let it steep 1 hour. Chill the tea.

**2** Remove the tea bag and add the tea, stevia, and muddled raspberries to a glass.

**3** Add the ice cubes. Serve immediately.

## Make This Into Lemonade

To make this caffeine-free drink into raspberry rooibos lemonade, add a squeeze of fresh lemon and more liquid stevia to taste.

# ROSEMARY LEMON ICED GREEN TEA

*With the antioxidants from green tea and the refreshing tang from lemon, this delicious keto drink has it all. Rosemary is an unusual herb pairing that somehow just works. You can also switch it up and use fresh thyme instead!*

**Serves 1**

**1 cup water**
**1 green tea bag**
**1 (4") sprig fresh rosemary**
**7 drops liquid stevia**
**2 slices fresh lemon**
**1 cup ice cubes**

**Per Serving**
Calories: 4 | Fat: 0g
Protein: 0g | Sodium: 4mg
Fiber: 0g | Carbohydrates: 0g
Net Carbohydrates: 0g | Sugar: 0g

**1** In a small saucepan, bring water to a boil and then pour it into a mug. Add the tea bag and rosemary sprig and let it steep 1 hour. Chill the tea.

**2** Remove the tea bag and rosemary sprig, and add the tea, stevia, lemon slices, and ice to a glass.

**3** Serve immediately.

# CARDAMOM PLUM ICED BLACK TEA

*Cardamom adds a bright, almost citrus-like flavor to this iced black tea. It's a lovely pairing with plum! If you don't have cardamom, you can use a pinch of Chinese five spice powder instead.*

**Serves 1**

**1 cup water**
**1 black tea bag**
**⅛ teaspoon ground cardamom**
**4 drops liquid stevia**
**¼ medium plum, thinly sliced**
**1 cup ice cubes**

**Per Serving**
Calories: 11 | Fat: 0g
Protein: 0g | Sodium: 8mg
Fiber: 0g | Carbohydrates: 3g
Net Carbohydrates: 3g | Sugar: 2g

**1** In a small saucepan, bring the water to a boil and then pour it into a mug. Add the tea bag and cardamom and let it steep 1 hour. Chill the tea.

**2** Remove the tea bag, and add the tea, stevia, plum, and ice to a glass.

**3** Serve immediately.

# CHAPTER 5

# JUICE

# WATERMELON LIME INFUSION

*Sweet watermelon and sour lime make a very refreshing combo. For a fun twist, freeze the watermelon balls. Note that each ¼ cup serving of fresh watermelon balls (which is about 39 grams) has 2.71g net carbs, which is on the high end for keto-friendly fruit. We recommend weighing your portions if accuracy in your macros is important to you!*

**Serves 1**

**1 cup water**
**¼ cup fresh watermelon balls**
**3 slices fresh lime**
**½ cup ice cubes**

**1** Add the water, watermelon balls, and lime slices to a glass.

**2** Add the ice.

**3** Serve.

**Per Serving**
Calories: 19 | Fat: 0g
Protein: 0g | Sodium: 1mg
Fiber: 1g | Carbohydrates: 5g
Net Carbohydrates: 5g | Sugar: 3g

## Can You Use a Different Kind of Melon?

Yes! Each ¼ cup of fresh honeydew balls (about 44 grams) has 3.62g net carbs. Alternatively, each ¼ cup of fresh cantaloupe balls (about 44 grams) has 3.21g net carbs.

# RASPBERRY LEMONADE

*Nothing is more refreshing than a tall glass of ice cold lemonade on a hot day! This keto version is pretty in pink, thanks to fresh red raspberries. You can muddle the berries if you want, or leave them whole for sweet/tart bursts of flavor.*

**Serves 1**

**1 cup water**
**1 tablespoon fresh lemon juice**
**7 drops liquid stevia**
**¼ cup fresh red raspberries**
**½ cup ice cubes**

**Per Serving**
Calories: 20 | Fat: 0g
Protein: 0g | Sodium: 2mg
Fiber: 2g | Carbohydrates: 5g
Net Carbohydrates: 3g | Sugar: 2g

**1** Add the water, lemon juice, and stevia to a glass.

**2** Add the raspberries and ice.

**3** Serve.

### Lemon Flavor Without the Sourness

To get the bright lemon flavor without all the lemon sourness, use fresh lemon zest instead of fresh lemon juice. For this recipe you can use 1 teaspoon fresh lemon zest for zippy flavor and skip the lemon juice.

# FAUX RED SANGRIA

*Traditional sangria is a Spanish drink that usually contains red wine, chopped fruit, and brandy. This fruity drink mimics the flavors with much fewer carbs and no alcohol so it's great for the whole family. It tastes like fruit punch!*

Serves 1

¾ cup water
1 tablespoon tart cherry juice
10 drops liquid stevia
1 slice fresh orange
¼ small plum, sliced
4 fresh blackberries
½ cup ice cubes
1 fresh cherry

**Per Serving**
Calories: 29 | Fat: 0g
Protein: 1g | Sodium: 4mg
Fiber: 1g | Carbohydrates: 7g
Net Carbohydrates: 5g | Sugar: 5g

**1** Add the water, cherry juice, and stevia to a glass and stir to combine.

**2** Add the orange slice, plum slices, blackberries, and ice.

**3** Place the cherry on top and serve.

## A Word on Adding Alcohol

Be mindful of the carb content if you want to add red wine to this recipe. We recommend using a dry red, such as a cabernet sauvignon, pinot noir, or merlot. If you decide to use wine, you can also dilute it with water to lower the carbs.

# FAUX SPARKLING WHITE SANGRIA

*White sangria is, as you probably guessed, the "white" version of red sangria, which is basically a wine-based fruit punch. White wine, brandy, and/or peach schnapps are classic components of white sangria, and this sparkling version has bubbles for an elegant twist!*

**Serves 1**

¾ cup sparkling water
5 drops liquid stevia
2 slices fresh orange
¼ small peach, sliced
½ cup ice cubes

**Per Serving**
Calories: 17 | Fat: 0g
Protein: 0g | Sodium: 39mg
Fiber: 1g | Carbohydrates: 4g
Net Carbohydrates: 4g | Sugar: 3g

**1** Add the sparkling water and stevia to a glass.

**2** Add the orange slices, peach slices, and ice. Stir.

**3** Serve.

# ELECTROLYTE LEMONADE

*If you want a more natural way to replenish electrolytes after an intense workout or on a hot day, this is the drink for you. We use a combination of coconut water, sea salt, and NoSalt as sources of magnesium, potassium, and sodium, which helps rehydrate you after sweating a lot. This is basically the keto version of Gatorade, and it tastes way better!*

**Serves 1**

½ cup coconut water
½ tablespoon fresh lemon juice
5 drops liquid stevia
⅛ teaspoon sea salt
⅛ teaspoon NoSalt Sodium-Free Salt
½ cup ice cubes

**Per Serving**
Calories: 25 | Fat: 0g
Protein: 1g | Sodium: 418mg
Fiber: 1g | Carbohydrates: 5g
Net Carbohydrates: 4g | Sugar: 3g

**1** Stir all ingredients together in a glass.

**2** Serve.

## What Is NoSalt?

NoSalt is a sodium-free salt alternative that contains potassium chloride. We use it in our electrolyte drinks for the potassium.

# ELECTROLYTE LIMEADE

*Just like our Electrolyte Lemonade, this Electrolyte Limeade is a great way to rehydrate after an intense workout or on a summer day when you're outside sweating a lot. You can bump up the citrus flavor even more by adding 1 teaspoon of fresh citrus zest!*

**Serves 1**

½ cup coconut water
½ tablespoon fresh lime juice
5 drops liquid stevia
⅛ teaspoon sea salt
⅛ teaspoon NoSalt Sodium-Free Salt
½ cup ice cubes

**1** Stir all ingredients together in a glass.

**2** Serve.

**Per Serving**
Calories: 25 | Fat: 0g | Protein: 1g | Sodium: 418mg | Fiber: 1g
Carbohydrates: 5g | Net Carbohydrates: 4g | Sugar: 3g

---

# PEACH BELLINI MOCKTAIL

*For the best peach flavor in this keto mocktail, use the ripest peach you can find. A tiny hint of vanilla intensifies the peach flavor. And of course a Bellini needs bubbly, so don't skip the sparkling water!*

**Serves 1**

¼ small fresh ripe peach, sliced
1 tablespoon MCT oil
8 drops liquid stevia
¼ teaspoon vanilla extract
¾ cup sparkling water, chilled

**1** Add the peach, MCT oil, stevia, and vanilla extract to a blender and process until smooth.

**2** Pour into a glass and gently stir in the sparkling water.

**3** Serve immediately.

**Per Serving**
Calories: 133 | Fat: 14g | Protein: 0g | Sodium: 40mg | Fiber: 1g
Carbohydrates: 4g | Net Carbohydrates: 3g | Sugar: 3g

# STRAWBERRY BASIL LEMONADE

*Strawberries and basil is an odd-sounding flavor combination that somehow just works. If you're looking for an elegant way to switch up lemonade, this is it! Also, for a fun flavor variation, try this with a sprig of fresh thyme instead of basil.*

Serves 1

**1 cup water**
**1 tablespoon fresh lemon juice**
**7 drops liquid stevia**
**¼ cup sliced fresh strawberries**
**3 fresh basil leaves**
**½ cup ice cubes**

**Per Serving**
Calories: 17 | Fat: 0g
Protein: 0g | Sodium: 2mg
Fiber: 1g | Carbohydrates: 4g
Net Carbohydrates: 3g | Sugar: 2g

**1** Add the water, lemon juice, and stevia to a glass.

**2** Add the strawberries, basil, and ice. Stir.

**3** Serve.

# CUCUMBER KIWI

*Sweet and zippy kiwi pairs well with the crispness of cucumber. Mix this keto drink up (everything except the ice) and let it chill in the refrigerator for a couple hours to amplify the flavors.*

**Serves 1**

**1 cup water**

**1 teaspoon fresh lemon juice**

**3 drops liquid stevia**

**¼ cup thinly sliced unpeeled cucumber**

**½ medium kiwi, peeled and sliced**

**½ cup ice cubes**

**Per Serving**
Calories: 26 | Fat: 0g
Protein: 1g | Sodium: 2mg
Fiber: 1g | Carbohydrates: 6g
Net Carbohydrates: 5g | Sugar: 4g

**1** Add the water, lemon juice, and stevia to a glass.

**2** Add the cucumber, kiwi, and ice.

**3** Serve.

### How to Peel Kiwi

To peel a kiwi, cut off both ends of the kiwi, and use a vegetable peeler to cut the peel off in strips. Alternatively, you can peel a kiwi with a spoon. To do so, cut off both ends of the kiwi, insert a spoon just under the kiwi's skin and slide it around to separate the flesh of the fruit from the skin.

# TART CHERRY VANILLA

*This nostalgic flavor is a keto twist on a classic soda. You can use vanilla bean paste instead of vanilla extract if you like the pretty black specks in your drink.*

**Serves 1**

1 cup sparkling water
7 drops liquid stevia
1 teaspoon tart cherry juice
½ teaspoon vanilla extract
½ cup ice cubes

**1** Add all ingredients to a glass.

**2** Serve.

**Per Serving**
Calories: 9 | Fat: 0g | Protein: 0g | Sodium: 52mg | Fiber: 0g
Carbohydrates: 1g | Net Carbohydrates: 1g | Sugar: 1g

---

# SPARKLING BLACKBERRY MINT SPLASH

*When you add berries and fresh herbs, you'll find that water is never boring! If you have trouble getting in your water requirements every day, start with a fun, fruity keto drink like this. You can also use ¼ cup frozen blackberries; just make sure to decrease the ice amount to ¼ cup.*

**Serves 1**

1 cup sparkling water
3 drops liquid stevia
¼ cup fresh blackberries
10 fresh mint leaves
½ cup ice cubes

**1** Add all ingredients to a glass.

**2** Serve.

**Per Serving**
Calories: 16 | Fat: 0g | Protein: 1g | Sodium: 52mg | Fiber: 2g
Carbohydrates: 4g | Net Carbohydrates: 2g | Sugar: 2g

# CUCUMBER MINT REFRESHER

*When it comes to hydration on a hot day, cucumber is the way to go. Drink this ketofied water post-workout to rehydrate your body, and while you're at it, add a pinch of sea salt to help replenish electrolytes. And save a couple cucumber slices to put on your eyes!*

**Serves 1**

1½ cups water

½ cup thinly sliced unpeeled cucumber

10 fresh mint leaves

½ cup ice cubes

**Per Serving**
Calories: 8 | Fat: 0g
Protein: 0g | Sodium: 1mg
Fiber: 0g | Carbohydrates: 2g
Net Carbohydrates: 2g | Sugar: 1g

**1** Add all ingredients to a glass.

**2** Serve.

# TRIPLE CITRUS—INFUSED WATER

*For this flavorful infusion, you can slice up the fruit and just start sipping. However, if you want the flavor even more concentrated, we recommend letting it sit in the refrigerator for a couple hours or overnight.*

**Serves 1**

**1 cup water**
**2 slices fresh orange**
**3 slices fresh lemon**
**3 slices fresh lime**
**½ cup ice cubes**

**1** Add all ingredients to a glass.

**2** Serve.

**Per Serving**
Calories: 28 | Fat: 0g | Protein: 1g | Sodium: 1mg | Fiber: 2g
Carbohydrates: 8g | Net Carbohydrates: 6g | Sugar: 4g

---

# BUBBLY BLUEBERRY GINGER WATER

*Although blueberries and ginger aren't a common pairing, there's just something about that combination that is completely delicious. Sweet/tart blueberries plus tangy/aromatic ginger equals perfect refreshment! Feel free to muddle the blueberries a bit before adding them to this drink if you want their flavor to permeate.*

**Serves 1**

**1 cup sparkling water**
**2 tablespoons Sweet Ginger Syrup (see Faux Ginger Ale recipe in this chapter)**
**¼ cup fresh blueberries**
**½ cup ice cubes**

**1** Gently stir together the sparkling water and Sweet Ginger Syrup in a glass.

**2** Add the blueberries and ice, and serve immediately.

**Per Serving**
Calories: 24 | Fat: 0g | Protein: 0g | Sodium: 51mg | Fiber: 1g
Carbohydrates: 32g | Net Carbohydrates: 5g | Sugar: 4g

# FAUX GINGER ALE

*Diet ginger ale will be a thing of the past once you try this recipe! Feel free to add more or less Sweet Ginger Syrup according to your taste preferences. You can also use this syrup to make keto-friendly versions of adult beverages, such as a Moscow mule. This syrup recipe yields about 10 tablespoons of syrup.*

**Serves 1**

**SWEET GINGER SYRUP**
1 (1½") piece fresh ginger, peeled and thinly sliced
¼ cup granulated erythritol
½ cup water

**GINGER ALE**
1 cup sparkling water
½ cup ice cubes

**Per Serving**
Calories: 2 | Fat: 0g
Protein: 0g | Sodium: 51mg
Fiber: 0g | Carbohydrates: 27g
Net Carbohydrates: 1g | Sugar: 0g
Sugar Alcohols: 27g

**1 For the Sweet Ginger Syrup:** Add all syrup ingredients to a small saucepan and bring to a boil. Once boiling, let it boil vigorously (turning the heat down a touch so it doesn't boil over), for 90 seconds. Remove from the heat. Cover the saucepan and let the ginger steep in the liquid 2 hours. Strain out and discard the ginger, and reserve the syrup for use.

**2 For the Ginger Ale:** Add the sparkling water and 2 tablespoons of Sweet Ginger Syrup to a glass and gently stir to combine (don't stir too much or you'll lose the bubbles). Add the ice and serve immediately.

**Prepare in Advance**

You can make the Sweet Ginger Syrup in advance and then use it to whip up this Faux Ginger Ale any time you have a craving. You can make the syrup up to one week in advance and store it covered in the refrigerator.

# PINEAPPLE BASIL–INFUSED WATER

*To enhance the flavor of this drink even more, you can add a little splash of vanilla extract or a lemon twist. We leave the pineapple in chunks and eat it as we drink this. However, if you prefer, you can first muddle (basically crush) the pineapple or purée it.*

**Serves 1**

**1½ cups water**
**¼ cup chopped pineapple**
**6 fresh basil leaves**
**½ cup ice cubes**

**Per Serving**
Calories: 21 | Fat: 0g
Protein: 0g | Sodium: 1mg
Fiber: 1g | Carbohydrates: 5g
Net Carbohydrates: 5g | Sugar: 4g

**1** Add all ingredients to a glass.
**2** Serve.

# DEEP GREENS CREAMY VANILLA COCONUT MILK

*If you don't have a juicer, it's still possible to make green juice using a blender. We blend kale with water and strain it through cheesecloth. If you don't have cheesecloth, you can strain the liquid twice through a fine mesh sieve. And if kale isn't your thing, use any dark leafy greens you like!*

**Serves 1**

**1½ cups baby kale**
**1 cup water**
**¼ cup canned unsweetened full-fat coconut milk**
**¾ teaspoon vanilla extract**
**¼ teaspoon fresh lemon juice**
**10 drops liquid stevia**
**½ cup ice cubes**

**Per Serving**
Calories: 133 | Fat: 12g
Protein: 2g | Sodium: 19mg
Fiber: 2g | Carbohydrates: 4g
Net Carbohydrates: 3g | Sugar: 1g

**1** Add the kale and water to a blender and process until smooth.

**2** Strain the kale liquid through a cheesecloth, or twice through a fine mesh sieve. Keep the liquid, and discard the pulp.

**3** Add the kale liquid, coconut milk, vanilla extract, lemon juice, and stevia to the blender and process until smooth.

**4** Pour into a glass and add the ice.

**5** Serve.

## What Kind of Coconut Milk Should You Use?

In almost all our keto drinks we prefer to use canned unsweetened full-fat coconut milk. Look for an organic, BPA-free product. Be sure to give it a stir before measuring because the thicker waxy portion rises to the top, and the thinner liquidy portion settles to the bottom.

# APPLE CINNAMON—INFUSED WATER

*This sweetly spiced keto drink has a very autumnal vibe! Don't skip the lemon juice here; it helps slow down the apple from oxidizing and turning brown.*

**Serves 1**

**1 cup water**

**¼ medium tart green apple (such as Granny Smith), cored and thinly sliced**

**½ teaspoon fresh lemon juice**

**⅛ teaspoon ground cinnamon**

**7 drops liquid stevia**

**½ cup ice cubes**

**Per Serving**
Calories: 25 | Fat: 0g
Protein: 0g | Sodium: 2mg
Fiber: 1g | Carbohydrates: 7g
Net Carbohydrates: 6g | Sugar: 5g

**1** Add all ingredients to a glass.

**2** Serve.

## Make It Ahead

This drink is a good one to make a day ahead of time. If you want to do so, we recommend using a small cinnamon stick instead of ground cinnamon to subtly infuse the water. Hold off on adding the ice until right before serving.

# KIWI ORANGE–INFUSED WATER

*To take this drink to the next level, stick two cloves in the peel of one of the orange slices, and let the orange and kiwi slices soak in the water overnight. The cloves make it a whole new flavor experience!*

**Serves 1**

**1 cup water**
**3 slices fresh orange**
**½ medium kiwi, peeled and sliced**
**½ cup ice cubes**

Per Serving
Calories: 45 | Fat: 0g
Protein: 1g | Sodium: 1mg
Fiber: 2g | Carbohydrates: 11g
Net Carbohydrates: 9g | Sugar: 8g

**1** Add all ingredients to a glass.

**2** Serve.

# CHAPTER 6

# MILKSHAKES

# ALMOND MILK

*This dairy-free milkshake is thick and rich with an ultra-creamy texture! We use almond milk as the base with almond butter and a little splash of almond extract to drive home the almond flavor. The great thing about this milkshake is you can swap out the almond butter for any flavor of nut butter you like to change up the flavor profile.*

**Serves 1**

1 cup plain unsweetened almond milk

2 tablespoons unsweetened creamy almond butter

½ tablespoon milled golden flaxseed

1 teaspoon vanilla extract

¼ teaspoon almond extract

10 drops liquid stevia

⅛ teaspoon sea salt

1 cup ice cubes

**Per Serving**
Calories: 265 | Fat: 22g
Protein: 9g | Sodium: 551mg
Fiber: 4g | Carbohydrates: 9g
Net Carbohydrates: 5g | Sugar: 3g

**1** Add the almond milk, almond butter, flaxseed, vanilla extract, almond extract, stevia, and salt to a blender and process until smooth.

**2** Add the ice cubes and pulse until thick and creamy, tamping down as necessary.

**3** Pour into a glass and serve immediately.

# BLUEBERRY CHOCOLATE CHIA

*Dark chocolate plus berries is one of our very favorite chocolate pairings. This decadent milkshake tastes like chocolate-covered blueberries and is sure to satisfy the sweetest of sweet tooth cravings. To make it even more decadent, top it with a dollop of whipped cream and a few dark chocolate shavings.*

Serves 1

¼ cup heavy whipping cream

½ cup water

1 tablespoon unsweetened cocoa powder

1 tablespoon chia seeds

12 drops liquid stevia

1 teaspoon vanilla extract

⅛ teaspoon sea salt

¼ cup frozen blueberries

¾ cup ice cubes

**Per Serving**
Calories: 314 | Fat: 26g
Protein: 5g | Sodium: 313mg
Fiber: 6g | Carbohydrates: 14g
Net Carbohydrates: 8g | Sugar: 6g

**1** Add the cream, water, cocoa powder, chia seeds, stevia, vanilla extract, and salt to a blender and process until smooth.

**2** Add the frozen blueberries and ice cubes and pulse until thick and creamy, tamping down as necessary.

**3** Pour into a glass and serve immediately.

## How Far Ahead Can You Make a Milkshake?

Many milkshakes are made with liquid blended with ice cubes, and therefore have a tendency to melt fairly quickly. We recommend finishing your milkshake within about 20 minutes after making it for the best taste and texture.

# VANILLA CARAMEL SWIRL

*The richness of creamy vanilla and the buttery, slightly nutty flavor of caramel are a match made in heaven! This milkshake combines them for a completely irresistible keto treat.*

Serves 1

1 tablespoon toasted almonds

¼ cup heavy whipping cream

½ cup water

1 teaspoon milled golden flaxseed

10 drops liquid stevia

1 teaspoon vanilla extract

1 teaspoon vanilla bean paste

⅛ teaspoon sea salt

1 cup ice cubes

2 tablespoons Homemade Keto Caramel (see Blended Cashew Vanilla Coffee recipe in Chapter 3)

**Per Serving**
Calories: 411 | Fat: 39g
Protein: 5g | Sodium: 344mg
Fiber: 2g | Carbohydrates: 10g
Net Carbohydrates: 6g | Sugar: 6g

**1** Add the almonds to a blender and pulse until powdery.

**2** Add the cream, water, flaxseed, stevia, vanilla extract, vanilla bean paste, and salt to the blender and process until smooth.

**3** Add the ice cubes and pulse until thick and creamy, tamping down as necessary.

**4** Pour into a glass, swirl in the Homemade Keto Caramel, and serve immediately.

# CANDIED ALMOND VANILLA

*With vanilla and cinnamon, this candied nut milkshake will make you feel like you're taking a trip to the state fairgrounds. There's no better aroma than candied almonds!*

**Serves 1**

### CANDIED ALMONDS
2 tablespoons almonds
½ teaspoon granulated monk fruit/erythritol blend
½ teaspoon vanilla extract
⅛ teaspoon sea salt

### MILKSHAKE
¼ cup heavy whipping cream
½ cup water
1 teaspoon milled golden flaxseed
10 drops liquid stevia
1 teaspoon vanilla extract
1 teaspoon vanilla bean paste
¼ teaspoon ground cinnamon
⅛ teaspoon sea salt
1 cup ice cubes

**Per Serving**
Calories: 320 | Fat: 28g
Protein: 5g | Sodium: 601mg
Fiber: 2g | Carbohydrates: 11g
Net Carbohydrates: 6g | Sugar: 6g

**1 For the Candied Almonds:** Add all the almond ingredients to a small nonstick skillet over medium heat. Cook until the nuts smell toasted, about 3–4 minutes. Cool completely.

**2 For the Milkshake:** Add the cream, water, flaxseed, stevia, vanilla extract, vanilla bean paste, cinnamon, and salt to a blender and process until smooth.

**3** Add the ice cubes and pulse until thick and creamy, tamping down as necessary.

**4** Add half of the candied almonds and pulse a couple times.

**5 To Serve:** Pour into a glass, sprinkle remaining candied almonds on top, and serve immediately.

# CANDIED PECAN VANILLA

*The pièce de résistance on this gorgeous vanilla-flecked milkshake is the candied pecans. They're slightly aromatic with vanilla and have the perfect level of sweetness. Just make sure you whip up a double batch because you'll be tempted to eat them all before you even start the milkshake!*

**Serves 1**

**CANDIED PECANS**
2 tablespoons shelled pecans
½ teaspoon granulated monk fruit/erythritol blend
½ teaspoon vanilla extract
⅛ teaspoon sea salt

**MILKSHAKE**
¼ cup heavy whipping cream
½ cup water
1 teaspoon milled golden flaxseed
10 drops liquid stevia
1 teaspoon vanilla extract
1 teaspoon vanilla bean paste
⅛ teaspoon sea salt
1 cup ice cubes

**Per Serving**
Calories: 346 | Fat: 32g
Protein: 3g | Sodium: 601mg
Fiber: 2g | Carbohydrates: 10g
Net Carbohydrates: 6g | Sugar: 6g

**1** **For the Candied Pecans:** Add all the pecan ingredients to a small nonstick skillet over medium heat. Cook until the nuts smell toasted, about 3–4 minutes. Cool completely.

**2** **For the Milkshake:** Add the cream, water, flaxseed, stevia, vanilla extract, vanilla bean paste, and salt to a blender and process until smooth.

**3** Add the ice cubes and pulse until thick and creamy, tamping down as necessary.

**4** Add half of the candied pecans and pulse a couple times.

**5** **To Serve:** Pour into a glass, sprinkle remaining candied pecans on top, and serve immediately.

# CARAMEL CHEESECAKE

*Imagine sitting down to a luscious slice of cheesecake dripping with caramel sauce...in milkshake form! This dessert-like treat tastes like the real deal, minus the carbs.*

**Serves 1**

**1 ounce cream cheese**

**¼ cup heavy whipping cream**

**½ cup water**

**2 tablespoons Homemade Keto Caramel (see Blended Cashew Vanilla Coffee recipe in Chapter 3)**

**½ teaspoon milled golden flaxseed**

**1 teaspoon vanilla extract**

**¼ teaspoon vanilla bean paste**

**⅛ teaspoon sea salt**

**10 drops liquid stevia**

**1 cup ice cubes**

**Per Serving**
Calories: 440 | Fat: 44g
Protein: 4g | Sodium: 432mg
Fiber: 0g | Carbohydrates: 8g
Net Carbohydrates: 5g | Sugar: 5g

**1** Add the cream cheese, cream, water, Homemade Keto Caramel, flaxseed, vanilla extract, vanilla bean paste, salt, and stevia to a blender and process until smooth.

**2** Add the ice cubes and pulse until thick and creamy, tamping down as necessary.

**3** Pour into a glass and serve immediately.

# CHOCOLATE CARAMEL

*So many of our milkshakes take their flavor profile inspiration from candy bars. If you like salted caramel, sprinkle a little flaky sea salt on top to enhance the flavor even more.*

**Serves 1**

1 tablespoon toasted almonds

3 tablespoons heavy whipping cream

2 tablespoons Homemade Keto Caramel (see Blended Cashew Vanilla Coffee recipe in Chapter 3)

½ cup water

1 tablespoon unsweetened cocoa powder

8 drops liquid stevia

1 teaspoon vanilla extract

¼ teaspoon espresso powder

⅛ teaspoon sea salt

1 cup ice cubes

**1** Add the almonds to a blender and pulse until powdery.

**2** Add the cream, Homemade Keto Caramel, water, cocoa powder, stevia, vanilla extract, espresso powder, and salt to the blender and process until smooth.

**3** Add the ice cubes and pulse until thick and creamy, tamping down as necessary.

**4** Pour into a glass and serve immediately.

**Per Serving**
Calories: 338 | Fat: 32g
Protein: 4g | Sodium: 339mg
Fiber: 2g | Carbohydrates: 9g
Net Carbohydrates: 4g | Sugar: 3g

# CHOCOLATE PEANUT BUTTER

*Just like a Reese's peanut butter cup, this chocolate plus peanut butter milkshake will satisfy your strongest candy cravings. If you didn't know this drink was keto, you'd never guess!*

**Serves 1**

1 tablespoon unsweetened natural peanut butter

¼ cup heavy whipping cream

½ cup water

1 tablespoon unsweetened cocoa powder

½ tablespoon chia seeds

12 drops liquid stevia

1 teaspoon vanilla extract

¼ teaspoon espresso powder

⅛ teaspoon sea salt

1 cup ice cubes

**Per Serving**
Calories: 364 | Fat: 33g
Protein: 7g | Sodium: 315mg
Fiber: 5g | Carbohydrates: 11g
Net Carbohydrates: 6g | Sugar: 4g

**1** Add the peanut butter, cream, water, cocoa powder, chia seeds, stevia, vanilla extract, espresso powder, and salt to a blender and process until smooth.

**2** Add the ice cubes and pulse until thick and creamy, tamping down as necessary.

**3** Pour into a glass and serve immediately.

**Why Add Chia Seeds to a Smoothie or Milkshake?**

Chia seeds act as a natural thickener in this milkshake, helping create a rich, creamy texture. An added bonus: Chia seeds are a good source of fiber, protein, and healthy fat!

# CHOCOLATE ALMOND JOY

*This is as close to an exact replica of the candy bar as we could get—and it's insanely close! There's no reason to feel deprived when you're following a low-carb and/or keto lifestyle. Candy bar cravings, be gone!*

**Serves 1**

1 tablespoon toasted almonds

2 tablespoons unsweetened shredded coconut

¼ cup heavy whipping cream

½ cup water

1 tablespoon unsweetened cocoa powder

12 drops liquid stevia

1 teaspoon vanilla extract

¼ teaspoon almond extract

⅛ teaspoon sea salt

1 cup ice cubes

**Per Serving**
Calories: 320 | Fat: 29g
Protein: 4g | Sodium: 313mg
Fiber: 3g | Carbohydrates: 8g
Net Carbohydrates: 5g | Sugar: 3g

**1** Add the almonds and coconut to a blender and pulse until powdery.

**2** Add the cream, water, cocoa powder, stevia, vanilla extract, almond extract, and salt to the blender and process until smooth.

**3** Add the ice cubes and pulse until thick and creamy, tamping down as necessary.

**4** Pour into a glass and serve immediately.

# CHOCOLATE CHEESECAKE

*If you can't decide between a slice of cheesecake or chocolate cake, now you don't have to! To enhance the flavor even more, add a spoonful of Homemade Keto Caramel and scale back a touch on the stevia.*

**Serves 1**

1 ounce cream cheese
¼ cup heavy whipping cream
½ cup water
1 tablespoon unsweetened cocoa powder
½ teaspoon milled golden flaxseed
1 teaspoon vanilla extract
¼ teaspoon vanilla bean paste
⅛ teaspoon sea salt
12 drops liquid stevia
1 cup ice cubes

**Per Serving**
Calories: 353 | Fat: 33g
Protein: 5g | Sodium: 400mg
Fiber: 2g | Carbohydrates: 8g
Net Carbohydrates: 6g | Sugar: 4g

**1** Add the cream cheese, cream, water, cocoa powder, flaxseed, vanilla extract, vanilla bean paste, salt, and stevia to a blender and process until smooth.

**2** Add the ice cubes and pulse until thick and creamy, tamping down as necessary.

**3** Pour into a glass and serve immediately.

# CHOCOLATE CRUNCH

*The slight bitterness of cacao nibs is a perfect balance to this smooth and creamy blended chocolate drink. If you find that cacao nibs are a little too bitter for you, go ahead and use stevia-sweetened chocolate chips instead.*

**Serves 1**

1 tablespoon toasted almonds
¼ cup heavy whipping cream
½ cup water
1 tablespoon unsweetened cocoa powder
12 drops liquid stevia
1 teaspoon vanilla extract
1 teaspoon fresh orange zest
⅛ teaspoon sea salt
1 cup ice cubes
2 teaspoons cacao nibs

**Per Serving**
Calories: 302 | Fat: 28g
Protein: 4g | Sodium: 311mg
Fiber: 3g | Carbohydrates: 8g
Net Carbohydrates: 5g | Sugar: 3g

**1** Add the almonds to a blender and pulse until powdery.

**2** Add the cream, water, cocoa powder, stevia, vanilla extract, orange zest, and salt to the blender and process until smooth.

**3** Add the ice cubes and pulse until thick and creamy, tamping down as necessary.

**4** Add the cacao nibs and pulse a few times.

**5** Pour into a glass and serve immediately.

# CHOCOLATE MINT

*Fans of mint chocolate chip ice cream, this keto milkshake is for you! We add a little bit of avocado to give it richness and creaminess, and also for added potassium and magnesium.*

Serves 1

3 tablespoons heavy whipping cream

¼ medium avocado, peeled, pitted, and sliced

½ cup water

1 tablespoon unsweetened cocoa powder

10 drops liquid stevia

1 teaspoon vanilla extract

¼ teaspoon mint extract

⅛ teaspoon sea salt

1 cup ice cubes

**Per Serving**
Calories: 275 | Fat: 25g
Protein: 3g | Sodium: 310mg
Fiber: 5g | Carbohydrates: 9g
Net Carbohydrates: 4g | Sugar: 2g

**1** Add the cream, avocado, water, cocoa powder, stevia, vanilla extract, mint extract, and salt to a blender and process until smooth.

**2** Add the ice cubes and pulse until thick and creamy, tamping down as necessary.

**3** Pour into a glass and serve immediately.

## Greens in a Milkshake?

Need to get some more greens into your diet? Put some in this milkshake! That's right, you can add up to ½ cup of baby spinach leaves to this milkshake and you won't even know they're there.

# PISTACHIO

*Would you believe there are actually store-bought low-carb pistachio ice creams that don't contain pistachios (or even pistachio extract) as an ingredient? They taste like vanilla ice cream! That's not the case with this pistachio milkshake. You can bump up the pistachio flavor even more by adding ¼ teaspoon of pistachio extract.*

Serves 1

**2 tablespoons unsalted shelled pistachios**

**¼ cup heavy whipping cream**

**½ cup water**

**1 teaspoon milled golden flaxseed**

**10 drops liquid stevia**

**1 teaspoon vanilla extract**

**1 teaspoon vanilla bean paste**

**⅛ teaspoon sea salt**

**1 cup ice cubes**

Per Serving
Calories: 344 | Fat: 30g
Protein: 5g | Sodium: 311mg
Fiber: 2g | Carbohydrates: 10g
Net Carbohydrates: 8g | Sugar: 6g

**1** Add the pistachios to a blender and pulse until powdery.

**2** Add the cream, water, flaxseed, stevia, vanilla extract, vanilla bean paste, and salt to the blender and process until smooth.

**3** Add the ice cubes and pulse until thick and creamy, tamping down as necessary.

**4** Pour into a glass and serve immediately.

# CHOCOLATE ORANGE

*Have you had those break-apart chocolate oranges around the holidays? This healthy milkshake is a play on those flavors, but without the subsequent sugar crash!*

**Serves 1**

1 tablespoon toasted almonds

¼ cup heavy whipping cream

½ cup water

1 tablespoon unsweetened cocoa powder

12 drops liquid stevia

1 teaspoon vanilla extract

1 teaspoon fresh orange zest

⅛ teaspoon sea salt

1 cup ice cubes

**Per Serving**
Calories: 277 | Fat: 26g
Protein: 4g | Sodium: 311mg
Fiber: 3g | Carbohydrates: 7g
Net Carbohydrates: 4g | Sugar: 3g

**1** Add the almonds to a blender and pulse until powdery.

**2** Add the cream, water, cocoa powder, stevia, vanilla extract, orange zest, and salt to the blender and process until smooth.

**3** Add the ice cubes and pulse until thick and creamy, tamping down as necessary.

**4** Pour into a glass and serve immediately.

**Can You Use Orange Extract Instead?**

Yes, you can substitute orange extract in place of the zest in this recipe. Just make sure to use less extract because it's more highly concentrated. This recipe calls for 1 teaspoon fresh orange zest, so start with ¼ teaspoon orange extract and work up from there.

# CHOCOLATE-COVERED COFFEE BEAN

*This milkshake uses our Chocolate Orange milkshake (see recipe in this chapter) as the base and adds coffee beans for crunch and bursts of coffee flavor! We recommend using organic beans in any roast that you would enjoy drinking. If you prefer, you can pulse in chocolate-covered coffee beans (instead of regular coffee beans); just be mindful of the carb count.*

**Serves 1**

1 tablespoon toasted almonds
¼ cup heavy whipping cream
½ cup water
1 tablespoon unsweetened cocoa powder
12 drops liquid stevia
1 teaspoon vanilla extract
1 teaspoon fresh orange zest
⅛ teaspoon sea salt
1 cup ice cubes
2 teaspoons coffee beans

**Per Serving**
Calories: 285 | Fat: 26g
Protein: 4g | Sodium: 313mg
Fiber: 3g | Carbohydrates: 8g
Net Carbohydrates: 5g | Sugar: 3g

**1** Add the almonds to a blender and pulse until powdery.

**2** Add the cream, water, cocoa powder, stevia, vanilla extract, orange zest, and salt to the blender and process until smooth.

**3** Add the ice cubes and pulse until thick and creamy, tamping down as necessary.

**4** Add the coffee beans and pulse a few times.

**5** Pour into a glass and serve immediately.

# STRAWBERRY

*For the most intense strawberry flavor, we recommend flash-freezing fresh strawberries for use throughout the year. They're perfect for making decadent-tasting low-carb smoothies and milkshakes! We don't recommend using artificial strawberry flavorings and extracts because they have a fake flavor and aroma.*

**Serves 1**

¼ cup heavy whipping cream

½ cup water

1 teaspoon milled golden flaxseed

10 drops liquid stevia

1½ teaspoons vanilla extract

⅛ teaspoon sea salt

½ cup frozen chopped strawberries

½ cup ice cubes

**Per Serving**
Calories: 261 | Fat: 23g
Protein: 2g | Sodium: 312mg
Fiber: 2g | Carbohydrates: 10g
Net Carbohydrates: 8g | Sugar: 6g

**1** Add the cream, water, flaxseed, stevia, vanilla extract, and salt to a blender and process until smooth.

**2** Add the frozen strawberries and ice cubes and pulse until thick and creamy, tamping down as necessary.

**3** Pour into a glass and serve immediately.

# CINNAMON CHEESECAKE

*This creamy cheesecake milkshake has cinnamon added to simulate a graham cracker crust! You can add a few chopped pecans or walnuts on top for a little crunch.*

**Serves 1**

**1 ounce cream cheese**
**¼ cup heavy whipping cream**
**½ cup water**
**½ teaspoon milled golden flaxseed**
**1 teaspoon vanilla extract**
**¼ teaspoon vanilla bean paste**
**½ teaspoon ground cinnamon**
**⅛ teaspoon sea salt**
**12 drops liquid stevia**
**1 cup ice cubes**

**Per Serving**
Calories: 330 | Fat: 32g
Protein: 4g | Sodium: 399mg
Fiber: 1g | Carbohydrates: 6g
Net Carbohydrates: 5g | Sugar: 4g

**1** Add the cream cheese, cream, water, flaxseed, vanilla extract, vanilla bean paste, cinnamon, salt, and stevia to a blender and process until smooth.

**2** Add the ice cubes and pulse until thick and creamy, tamping down as necessary.

**3** Pour into a glass and serve immediately.

# PANCAKES AND SYRUP

*There are two secret components that make this Pancakes and Syrup milkshake actually taste like the real deal: a spice called fenugreek and a pinch of baking soda. Fenugreek is actually an ingredient in artificial maple syrup that has natural notes of caramel and maple. You can find it at just about any spice shop or online.*

Serves 1

⅔ cup water

3 tablespoons heavy whipping cream

2 tablespoons almond flour

2 tablespoons Homemade Keto Caramel (see Blended Cashew Vanilla Coffee recipe in Chapter 3)

½ tablespoon milled golden flaxseed

1 teaspoon vanilla extract

½ teaspoon ground cinnamon

¼ teaspoon fenugreek

7 drops liquid stevia

⅛ teaspoon sea salt

1/16 teaspoon baking soda

1 cup ice cubes

**1** Add the water, cream, almond flour, Homemade Keto Caramel, flaxseed, vanilla extract, cinnamon, fenugreek, stevia, salt, and baking soda to a blender and process until smooth.

**2** Add the ice cubes and pulse until thick and creamy, tamping down as necessary.

**3** Pour into a glass and serve immediately.

**Per Serving**
Calories: 371 | Fat: 63g
Protein: 5g | Sodium: 418mg
Fiber: 3g | Carbohydrates: 10g
Net Carbohydrates: 4g | Sugar: 3g

## Can You Use Maple-Flavored Syrup Instead?

You can use 1 tablespoon stevia-sweetened maple-flavored syrup here instead of fenugreek. If you do so, skip the liquid stevia and just add it to taste because it might be sweet enough without any added stevia!

# RASPBERRY VANILLA BEAN

*Here the sweet/tartness of raspberries brightens up the vanilla bean base. We like to use frozen raspberries so we can use less ice, and the resulting milkshake has a more highly concentrated flavor. You could also use fresh raspberries; just increase the ice cube amount to 1 cup.*

**Serves 1**

1 tablespoon toasted almonds

¼ cup heavy whipping cream

½ cup water

1 teaspoon milled golden flaxseed

10 drops liquid stevia

1 teaspoon vanilla extract

1 teaspoon vanilla bean paste

⅛ teaspoon sea salt

½ cup frozen red raspberries

½ cup ice cubes

**Per Serving**
Calories: 316 | Fat: 26g
Protein: 4g | Sodium: 311mg
Fiber: 6g | Carbohydrates: 15g
Net Carbohydrates: 9g | Sugar: 8g

**1** Add the almonds to a blender and pulse until powdery.

**2** Add the cream, water, flaxseed, stevia, vanilla extract, vanilla bean paste, and salt to the blender and process until smooth.

**3** Add the frozen raspberries and ice cubes and pulse until thick and creamy, tamping down as necessary.

**4** Pour into a glass and serve immediately.

# PECAN CARAMEL CHOCOLATE

*Instead of heading to a local ice cream shop, make this milkshake with your kiddos. No one will guess that this is healthy! For an ice cream shop feel, top with a dollop of whipped cream and a fresh cherry.*

**Serves 1**

**1 tablespoon toasted pecans**

**3 tablespoons heavy whipping cream**

**2 tablespoons Homemade Keto Caramel (see Blended Cashew Vanilla Coffee recipe in Chapter 3)**

**½ cup water**

**1 tablespoon unsweetened cocoa powder**

**8 drops liquid stevia**

**1 teaspoon vanilla extract**

**⅛ teaspoon sea salt**

**1 cup ice cubes**

**Per Serving**
Calories: 351 | Fat: 35g
Protein: 3g | Sodium: 339mg
Fiber: 2g | Carbohydrates: 8g
Net Carbohydrates: 4g | Sugar: 3g

**1** Add the pecans to a blender and pulse until powdery.

**2** Add the cream, Homemade Keto Caramel, water, cocoa powder, stevia, vanilla extract, and salt to the blender and process until smooth.

**3** Add the ice cubes and pulse until thick and creamy, tamping down as necessary.

**4** Pour into a glass and serve immediately.

# TOASTED COCONUT VANILLA

*Toasted coconut flakes act as the base flavor for this decadent coconutty keto milkshake! If you really want to make it something special, you can top it with a dollop of freshly whipped cream and an extra sprinkle of toasted coconut flakes. Add a cute red and white striped straw, and you'll think you're at a local ice cream parlor.*

Serves 1

**2 tablespoons unsweetened toasted coconut flakes**

**¼ cup heavy whipping cream**

**½ cup water**

**1 teaspoon milled golden flaxseed**

**10 drops liquid stevia**

**1 teaspoon vanilla extract**

**¼ teaspoon vanilla bean paste**

**¼ teaspoon coconut extract**

**⅛ teaspoon sea salt**

**1 cup ice cubes**

Per Serving
Calories: 302 | Fat: 29g
Protein: 3g | Sodium: 314mg
Fiber: 2g | Carbohydrates: 6g
Net Carbohydrates: 4g | Sugar: 4g

**1** Add the toasted coconut to a blender and pulse until powdery.

**2** Add the cream, water, flaxseed, stevia, vanilla extract, vanilla bean paste, coconut extract, and salt to the blender and process until smooth.

**3** Add the ice cubes and pulse until thick and creamy, tamping down as necessary.

**4** Pour into a glass and serve immediately.

## How to Toast Coconut on the Stovetop

To toast your coconut on the stovetop, first add the coconut flakes to a small nonstick skillet over medium-low heat. Continue cooking until they turn light golden brown and smell nutty, stirring frequently. Once toasted, transfer the coconut to a bowl to cool because it'll burn if you leave it in the hot skillet.

# VANILLA ORANGE CREAM

*We took a cue here from one of our favorite frozen treats as kids. It's a perfect balance of sunshiny, sweet/tart citrus and rich, creamy vanilla flavors. One sip, and you won't believe that this delicious treat is keto!*

**Serves 1**

**1 tablespoon toasted almonds**

**¼ cup heavy whipping cream**

**½ cup water**

**1 teaspoon milled golden flaxseed**

**10 drops liquid stevia**

**1 tablespoon fresh orange zest**

**1 teaspoon vanilla extract**

**1 teaspoon vanilla bean paste**

**⅛ teaspoon sea salt**

**1 cup ice cubes**

**Per Serving**
Calories: 282 | Fat: 26g
Protein: 3g | Sodium: 310mg
Fiber: 2g | Carbohydrates: 8g
Net Carbohydrates: 6g | Sugar: 5g

**1** Add the almonds to a blender and pulse until powdery.

**2** Add the cream, water, flaxseed, stevia, orange zest, vanilla extract, vanilla bean paste, and salt to the blender and process until smooth.

**3** Add the ice cubes and pulse until thick and creamy, tamping down as necessary.

**4** Pour into a glass and serve immediately.

**Does It Matter What Kind of Orange You Use for Zest?**

We like to use organic navel oranges when we're using the zest. Give them a good rinse first, and be sure not to zest too far down into the white pith, which can be bitter.

# VANILLA BEAN

*Those pretty little flecks of vanilla bean in this milkshake tell you right away that you're going to get deep vanilla flavor! If you don't have vanilla bean paste on hand you can double the amount of vanilla extract, but of course it won't have those gorgeous vanilla specks. The toasted almonds are here to add a subtle hint of nutty base flavor to the vanilla profile.*

**Serves 1**

**1 tablespoon toasted almonds**

**¼ cup heavy whipping cream**

**½ cup water**

**1 teaspoon milled golden flaxseed**

**10 drops liquid stevia**

**1 teaspoon vanilla extract**

**1 teaspoon vanilla bean paste**

**⅛ teaspoon sea salt**

**1 cup ice cubes**

**1** Add the almonds to a blender and pulse until powdery.

**2** Add the cream, water, flaxseed, stevia, vanilla extract, vanilla bean paste, and salt to the blender and process until smooth.

**3** Add the ice cubes and pulse until thick and creamy, tamping down as necessary.

**4** Pour into a glass and serve immediately.

**Per Serving**
Calories: 279 | Fat: 26g
Protein: 3g | Sodium: 310mg
Fiber: 1g | Carbohydrates: 7g
Net Carbohydrates: 5g | Sugar: 5g

## What Is Vanilla Bean Paste?

Vanilla bean paste contains the vanilla that's scraped from the inside of a vanilla bean pod in a sweet, thick liquid. It adds intensely deep vanilla flavor and pretty vanilla flecks.

# CHAPTER 7

# BROTHS

# PORK BONE BROTH BASE

*This Pork Bone Broth Base works well anywhere you'd normally use beef or chicken bone broth. You can use it to make a mean bowl of ramen. Zucchini noodles work well in it too!*

**Yields 4½ quarts**

**3 pounds pork bones**
**5 quarts water**
**2 teaspoons sea salt**
**1 teaspoon ground black pepper**
**1 tablespoon apple cider vinegar**
**4 small cloves garlic, smashed**
**1 medium yellow onion, quartered**

Per Serving (1 cup)
Calories: 44 | Fat: 0g
Protein: 7g | Sodium: 366mg
Fiber: 1g | Carbohydrates: 3g
Net Carbohydrates: 2g | Sugar: 2g

**1** Use the slow cooker function on an electric pressure cooker; add all ingredients and cook 8 hours.

**2** Press the Cancel button then press Manual, High Pressure and cook another 2 hours.

**3** Let the pressure naturally release and remove the lid.

**4** Strain bones and vegetables out of broth and discard. Taste and add additional salt and pepper if desired.

**5** Pour into six 24-ounce glass Mason jars.

**6** Cool completely and then store in the refrigerator up to three days.

## Should You Peel and Chop the Vegetables?

You don't need to peel the vegetables when you make bone broths, and you don't need to be particular about the way you chop them because the vegetables will be strained out. For example, we quarter a whole (unpeeled) onion and use it like that. For that reason, we recommend using organic vegetables.

# BBQ PORK BROTH

*If you're limiting calories but really want BBQ pork, this sippable broth is for you! The BBQ spices paired with the sweet and tangy flavor of this drink will make you think you're diving into a BBQ pork sammy.*

Serves 1

1 cup hot Pork Bone Broth Base (see recipe in this chapter)
1 tablespoon salted butter
1 teaspoon tomato paste
½ teaspoon apple cider vinegar
¼ teaspoon cumin
¼ teaspoon chili powder
⅛ teaspoon ground black pepper
⅛ teaspoon cayenne pepper
1 drop liquid stevia

**Per Serving**
Calories: 159 | Fat: 12g
Protein: 8g | Sodium: 391mg
Fiber: 2g | Carbohydrates: 5g
Net Carbohydrates: 3g | Sugar: 3g

**1** Add all ingredients to a blender and process until smooth.
**2** Serve.

# BEEF BONE BROTH BASE

*This method for making bone broth yields the most gelatinous result that's rich in gelatin and collagen and good for gut health and immune system function, as well as hair, nails, skin, and joints. For even more depth of flavor, you can roast the bones first. We try to enjoy a hot mug of sippable bone broth every day!*

**Yields 4½ quarts**

**3 pounds beef bones**
**5 quarts water**
**2 teaspoons sea salt**
**1 teaspoon ground black pepper**
**1 tablespoon apple cider vinegar**
**4 small cloves garlic, smashed**
**1 medium yellow onion, quartered**
**½ bunch parsley**

**Per Serving (1 cup)**
Calories: 61 | Fat: 1g
Protein: 10g | Sodium: 384mg
Fiber: 1g | Carbohydrates: 4g
Net Carbohydrates: 3g | Sugar: 3g

**1** Use the slow cooker function on an electric pressure cooker; add all ingredients and cook 8 hours.

**2** Press the Cancel button then press Manual, High Pressure and cook another 2 hours.

**3** Let the pressure naturally release and remove the lid.

**4** Strain bones and vegetables out of broth and discard. Taste and add additional salt and pepper if desired.

**5** Pour into six 24-ounce glass Mason jars. Cool completely, and then store in the refrigerator up to three days.

## How Can You Make This on the Stovetop?

You can make bone broth on the stovetop, but it will take much longer, up to three days. You'll need to keep an eye on it and add additional water to keep the bones covered. The broth is done when the bones are falling apart at the joints.

# HUNGARIAN BEEF BONE BROTH

*The combination of paprika and caraway gives this broth its signature Hungarian stew flavor, so don't skip them! This sipping broth is rich and hearty, and if you have beef on hand you can cook it up and add it to this broth to increase the protein.*

### Serves 1

**1 cup hot Beef Bone Broth Base (see recipe in this chapter)**
**1 tablespoon salted butter**
**1 small clove garlic, peeled**
**½ teaspoon sweet paprika**
**⅛ teaspoon caraway seeds**
**⅛ teaspoon ground black pepper**

**Per Serving**
Calories: 172 | Fat: 12g
Protein: 11g | Sodium: 389mg
Fiber: 2g | Carbohydrates: 6g
Net Carbohydrates: 4g | Sugar: 3g

**1** Add all ingredients to a blender and process until smooth.

**2** Serve.

### Can You Use Garlic Powder Instead?

Yes! You can omit the small clove of garlic and use ⅛–¼ teaspoon garlic powder instead. Don't use garlic salt, because that will make the end result too salty.

# CHICKEN BONE BROTH BASE

*There isn't much that a cup of chicken soup can't fix! With this base recipe up your sleeve, you're that much closer to the best homemade soup you've ever had.*

**Yields 4½ quarts**

**3 pounds chicken bones**
**5 quarts water**
**2 teaspoons sea salt**
**1 teaspoon ground black pepper**
**1 tablespoon apple cider vinegar**
**4 small cloves garlic, smashed**
**1 medium yellow onion, quartered**
**2 medium carrots, chopped**
**1 medium stalk celery, chopped**

**Per Serving (1 cup)**
Calories: 27 | Fat: 0g
Protein: 4g | Sodium: 348mg
Fiber: 1g | Carbohydrates: 2g
Net Carbohydrates: 1g | Sugar: 1g

**1** Use the slow cooker function on an electric pressure cooker; add all ingredients and cook 8 hours.

**2** Press the Cancel button then press Manual, High Pressure and cook another 2 hours.

**3** Let the pressure naturally release and remove the lid.

**4** Strain bones and vegetables out of broth and discard. Taste and add additional salt and pepper if desired.

**5** Pour into six 24-ounce glass Mason jars. Cool completely, and then store in the refrigerator up to three days.

# GARLIC AND HERB VEGETABLE BROTH

*As far as satisfying, easy broth drinks, this one is the gold standard! It's loaded with nutrients, and you can add protein in the form of cooked, chopped chicken or beef if you want. It's also delicious with 1 teaspoon of tomato paste blended in.*

**Serves 1**

**1 cup hot Vegetable Broth (see recipe in this chapter)**
**1 tablespoon salted butter**
**1 small clove garlic, peeled**
**¼ teaspoon dried Italian herbs**

**1** Add all ingredients to a blender and process until smooth.

**2** Serve.

**Per Serving**
Calories: 119 | Fat: 12g | Protein: 1g | Sodium: 320mg | Fiber: 3g
Carbohydrates: 4g | Net Carbohydrates: 1g | Sugar: 3g

---

# THAI CHICKEN BROTH

*Garlic, ginger, and coconut aminos add delicious savory flavor to this sipping broth. Make this a satisfying meal by adding leftover cooked chicken for protein and serve it garnished with a few leaves of freshly torn Thai basil to bump up the flavor!*

**Serves 1**

**1 cup hot Chicken Bone Broth Base (see recipe in this chapter)**
**1 tablespoon unsalted butter**
**1 small clove garlic, peeled**
**½ teaspoon coconut aminos**
**¼ teaspoon grated fresh ginger**
**⅛ teaspoon fish sauce**
**⅛ teaspoon ground black pepper**

**1** Add all ingredients to a blender and process until smooth.

**2** Serve.

**Per Serving**
Calories: 137 | Fat: 12g | Protein: 5g | Sodium: 453mg | Fiber: 1g
Carbohydrates: 4g | Net Carbohydrates: 3g | Sugar: 1g

# MEXICAN CHICKEN BROTH

*This craveable and sippable broth tastes just like tortilla soup, and you won't even miss the carbs! We use chili powder here (not chile powder), which is a spice blend that usually contains chile powder, paprika, cumin, Mexican oregano, and garlic powder. Look for a blend that doesn't contain sugar or thickeners.*

**Serves 1**

**1 cup hot Chicken Bone Broth Base (see recipe in this chapter)**

**1 tablespoon salted butter**

**1 teaspoon tomato paste**

**¼ teaspoon cumin**

**¼ teaspoon dried oregano**

**¼ teaspoon chili powder**

**⅛ teaspoon ground black pepper**

**Per Serving**
Calories: 138 | Fat: 12g
Protein: 5g | Sodium: 372mg
Fiber: 2g | Carbohydrates: 4g
Net Carbohydrates: 3g | Sugar: 1g

**1** Add all ingredients to a blender and process until smooth.

**2** Serve.

## Make It a Meal

Are you looking to turn this broth into a satisfying and tasty meal? That's easy to do! Add ½ cup cooked, shredded chicken and a sprinkle of cilantro on top and voilà: You have a delicious cup of soup.

# ITALIAN TOMATO AND HERB BEEF BONE BROTH

*This tastes like homemade slow-simmered tomato soup! It makes a great weekday lunch, and if you have a small blender (such as a Magic Bullet) you can whip it up at the office. If you want to take it to the next level, add a small handful of crumbled goat cheese and a few fresh basil leaves.*

**Serves 1**

**1 cup hot Beef Bone Broth Base (see recipe in this chapter)**
**1 tablespoon salted butter**
**1 small clove garlic, peeled**
**1 teaspoon tomato paste**
**¼ teaspoon dried Italian herbs**

**Per Serving**
Calories: 172 | Fat: 12g
Protein: 11g | Sodium: 388mg
Fiber: 1g | Carbohydrates: 6g
Net Carbohydrates: 5g | Sugar: 4g

**1** Add all ingredients to a blender and process until smooth.

**2** Serve.

## Make It Vegan

This recipe is easily converted to a vegan drink by simply skipping the Beef Bone Broth Base and using Vegetable Broth instead. You'll also want to use 1 tablespoon MCT oil in place of the butter.

# LEMON PEPPER CHICKEN BROTH

*Lemon and black pepper is a classic flavor combination for roast chicken. It's no surprise that this traditional roast chicken flavor is also delicious as a hot sipping broth! Feel free to adjust the amount of lemon juice and black pepper up or down to suit your personal preference.*

**Serves 1**

**1 cup hot Chicken Bone Broth Base (see recipe in this chapter)**

**1 tablespoon salted butter**

**½ teaspoon fresh lemon juice**

**⅛ teaspoon ground black pepper**

**Per Serving**
Calories: 130 | Fat: 12g
Protein: 5g | Sodium: 349mg
Fiber: 1g | Carbohydrates: 3g
Net Carbohydrates: 2g | Sugar: 1g

**1** Add all ingredients to a blender and process until smooth.

**2** Serve.

## What Fresh Herbs Would Go Well Here?

Lemon pepper provides a nice base flavor for this broth, but we like ours with added fresh herbs if we have them on hand. With this chicken broth you could also use fresh rosemary, thyme, sage, or parsley, or any combination of these herbs.

# CHINESE PORK BROTH

*This broth drink has a balanced profile, with freshness from ginger, acid from vinegar, saltiness from coconut aminos, and complexity from Chinese five spice powder. You can add a small clove of garlic too if you like.*

**Serves 1**

**1 cup hot Pork Bone Broth Base (see recipe in this chapter)**

**1 tablespoon unsalted butter**

**½ teaspoon coconut aminos**

**½ teaspoon grated fresh ginger**

**½ teaspoon rice wine vinegar**

**⅛ teaspoon Chinese five spice powder**

**⅛ teaspoon ground black pepper**

**Per Serving**
Calories: 150 | Fat: 12g
Protein: 7g | Sodium: 412mg
Fiber: 1g | Carbohydrates: 4g
Net Carbohydrates: 3g | Sugar: 2g

**1** Add all ingredients to a blender and process until smooth.

**2** Serve.

# MISO CHICKEN BROTH

*Miso is a Japanese fermented soybean paste that adds a huge punch of umami flavor. White miso is a bit milder and slightly sweeter than darker miso pastes, but you could also use yellow miso paste if that's what you can find or prefer. Look for miso paste in the international aisle of your local grocery store or online.*

**Serves 1**

1 cup hot **Chicken Bone Broth Base (see recipe in this chapter)**

1 tablespoon **unsalted butter**

1¼ teaspoons **white miso paste**

⅛ teaspoon **ground black pepper**

**Per Serving**
Calories: 143 | Fat: 12g
Protein: 5g | Sodium: 545mg
Fiber: 1g | Carbohydrates: 5g
Net Carbohydrates: 4g | Sugar: 2g

**1** Add all ingredients to a blender and process until smooth.

**2** Serve.

## Isn't Miso Paste High in Carbs?

Yes, miso paste has soybeans, and yes, soybeans are higher in carbs. Here we're using just 1¼ teaspoons of miso paste, which is plenty to flavor this delicious hot drink. Be sure to check the brand of miso paste you're using, but most brands contain 1g net carbs per 1 teaspoon serving. Just be mindful of your portion!

# PHO BEEF BONE BROTH

*Sipping on this complex-flavored savory hot broth, you'll think you walked into your favorite Vietnamese pho restaurant! Chinese five spice powder can be potent, so don't overdo it; but you need it for depth of flavor, so don't skip it either. Sprinkle a few fresh cilantro leaves on top of this broth to complete the experience.*

**Serves 1**

**1 cup hot Beef Bone Broth Base (see recipe in this chapter)**
**1 tablespoon unsalted butter**
**1 small clove garlic, peeled**
**½ teaspoon grated fresh ginger**
**½ teaspoon coconut aminos**
**½ teaspoon fresh lime juice**
**⅛ teaspoon fish sauce**
**⅛ teaspoon Chinese five spice powder**

**Per Serving**
Calories: 171 | Fat: 12g
Protein: 11g | Sodium: 489mg
Fiber: 1g | Carbohydrates: 6g
Net Carbohydrates: 5g | Sugar: 4g

**1** Add all ingredients to a blender and process until smooth.

**2** Serve.

**Want Some Noodles in Your Pho?**

It might sound basic, but our favorite keto-friendly noodles are actually spiralized zucchini, aka zoodles! There's no need to even cook them because we like their "al dente" texture; just add raw zoodles to hot broth and you're all set.

# VEGETABLE BROTH

*You'll be surprised at how flavorful and richly colored this Vegetable Broth is! You can use it as the base for any number of soups, or to make one of our favorite desk lunches, a cup of Garlic and Herb Vegetable Broth (see recipe in this chapter).*

**Yields 4½ quarts**

**5 quarts water**
**2 teaspoons sea salt**
**1 teaspoon ground black pepper**
**1 tablespoon apple cider vinegar**
**2 tablespoons extra-virgin olive oil**
**8 small cloves garlic, smashed**
**2 large tomatoes, quartered**
**2 medium yellow onions, quartered**
**4 medium carrots, chopped**
**3 medium stalks celery, chopped**
**1 medium rutabaga, chopped**
**1 bunch fresh parsley**
**10 sprigs fresh rosemary**
**10 sprigs fresh thyme**

Per Serving (1 cup)
Calories: 12 | Fat: 0g
Protein: 0g | Sodium: 318mg
Fiber: 2g | Carbohydrates: 3g
Net Carbohydrates: 0g | Sugar: 3g

**1** Add all ingredients to an electric pressure cooker. Press the Manual, High Pressure button and cook 2 hours.

**2** Let the pressure naturally release and remove the lid.

**3** Strain vegetables out of broth and discard. Taste and add additional salt and pepper if desired.

**4** Pour into six 24-ounce glass Mason jars.

**5** Cool completely and then store in the refrigerator up to three days.

## Should You Peel the Onions?

We recommend leaving the peels on the onion when making broth because they help give it a gorgeous golden color! For this reason, we like to use organic onions.

# US/METRIC CONVERSION CHART

## VOLUME CONVERSIONS

| US Volume Measure | Metric Equivalent |
|---|---|
| ⅛ teaspoon | 0.5 milliliter |
| ¼ teaspoon | 1 milliliter |
| ½ teaspoon | 2 milliliters |
| 1 teaspoon | 5 milliliters |
| ½ tablespoon | 7 milliliters |
| 1 tablespoon (3 teaspoons) | 15 milliliters |
| 2 tablespoons (1 fluid ounce) | 30 milliliters |
| ¼ cup (4 tablespoons) | 60 milliliters |
| ⅓ cup | 90 milliliters |
| ½ cup (4 fluid ounces) | 125 milliliters |
| ⅔ cup | 160 milliliters |
| ¾ cup (6 fluid ounces) | 180 milliliters |
| 1 cup (16 tablespoons) | 250 milliliters |
| 1 pint (2 cups) | 500 milliliters |
| 1 quart (4 cups) | 1 liter (about) |

## WEIGHT CONVERSIONS

| US Weight Measure | Metric Equivalent |
|---|---|
| ½ ounce | 15 grams |
| 1 ounce | 30 grams |
| 2 ounces | 60 grams |
| 3 ounces | 85 grams |
| ¼ pound (4 ounces) | 115 grams |
| ½ pound (8 ounces) | 225 grams |
| ¾ pound (12 ounces) | 340 grams |
| 1 pound (16 ounces) | 454 grams |

## OVEN TEMPERATURE CONVERSIONS

| Degrees Fahrenheit | Degrees Celsius |
|---|---|
| 200 degrees F | 95 degrees C |
| 250 degrees F | 120 degrees C |
| 275 degrees F | 135 degrees C |
| 300 degrees F | 150 degrees C |
| 325 degrees F | 160 degrees C |
| 350 degrees F | 180 degrees C |
| 375 degrees F | 190 degrees C |
| 400 degrees F | 205 degrees C |
| 425 degrees F | 220 degrees C |
| 450 degrees F | 230 degrees C |

## BAKING PAN SIZES

| American | Metric |
|---|---|
| 8 x 1½ inch round baking pan | 20 x 4 cm cake tin |
| 9 x 1½ inch round baking pan | 23 x 3.5 cm cake tin |
| 11 x 7 x 1½ inch baking pan | 28 x 18 x 4 cm baking tin |
| 13 x 9 x 2 inch baking pan | 30 x 20 x 5 cm baking tin |
| 2 quart rectangular baking dish | 30 x 20 x 3 cm baking tin |
| 15 x 10 x 2 inch baking pan | 30 x 25 x 2 cm baking tin (Swiss roll tin) |
| 9 inch pie plate | 22 x 4 or 23 x 4 cm pie plate |
| 7 or 8 inch springform pan | 18 or 20 cm springform or loose bottom cake tin |
| 9 x 5 x 3 inch loaf pan | 23 x 13 x 7 cm or 2 lb narrow loaf or pate tin |
| 1½ quart casserole | 1.5 liter casserole |
| 2 quart casserole | 2 liter casserole |

# INDEX